Family Assessment Form

Family Assessment Form

A Practice-Based Approach to Assessing Family Functioning

Children's Bureau of Southern California
CWLA Press • Washington, DC

CWLA Press is an imprint of the Child Welfare League of America, Inc.

© 1997 by the Children's Bureau of Southern California.

CHILD WELFARE LEAGUE OF AMERICA, INC.
440 First Street, NW, Third Floor, Washington, DC 20001–2085
Email: books@cwla.org

CURRENT PRINTING (last digit)
10 9 8 7 6 5 4 3 2 1

Cover design by Sarah Knipschild
Text design by Jennifer M. Price

Printed in the United States of America

ISBN # 0–87868–688–6

Library of Congress Cataloging-in-Publication Data
Family Assessment form : a practice-based approach to assessing
    family functioning / Children's Bureau of Southern California.
        p.   cm.
    ISBN 0-87868-688-6 (pbk.)
    1. Family social work–United States–Evaluation. 2. Family
    assessment–United States–Evaluation. 3. Evaluation research
    (Social action programs)–United States. 4. Children's Bureau of
    Southern California–Forms.   I. Children's Bureau of Southern
    California.
    HV699.F28   1997   97-13458
    362.82'0973–dc21   CIP

Contents

Introduction and Instructions*

Jacquelyn McCroskey, Alexandra Sladen, and William Meezan

The Family Assessment Form (FAF) was initially developed at the Children's Bureau of Southern California between 1985 and 1987 as a practice-based instrument to help child welfare practitioners standardize the assessment of family functioning and service planning for families receiving home-based services. Since then, it has been used with innumerable families in many different program settings (including community-based and office-based programs) in agencies all over the world. Since its initial development, the FAF has been modified and updated several times over the last decade based on the feedback and suggestions of families and practitioners. Its use in several research studies, both as an observational tool and a guide for a research interview, has provided additional information about its optimum format, length, and structure, as well as about its validity and reliability.

Unlike many other standardized instruments which are often used for research purposes, the FAF can and should be adapted to meet the needs of practitioners in specific program and agency settings. Indeed, we suggest that practitioners in each agency be encouraged to review the instrument and to modify it when necessary to best meet their needs and those of the families they serve. Entire sections may be deleted if they are not needed or if they are inappropriate for a particular program or client population. While we encourage maintaining the integrity of the six areas of family functioning as written, items within sections may be added to meet specific information needs, and whole new sections can be designed by agency practitioners to enhance their assessment within their service context. Changes to the "outcomes" sections of the FAF may affect the reliability and validity of the instrument if it is being used as a formal research instrument, though they will not change the basic purpose of the instrument or the way in which it is used.

Because of the developmental process undertaken at Children's Bureau, the continual adaptation of the FAF to meet workers needs, and the continual use of the FAF as an integral part of practice, research and evaluation are now ongoing methods of discovery at the Children's Bureau. Answering questions of program effectiveness has become an integral part of the culture of the agency, and is consistently embraced because it has been shown to enhance learning and program quality. And the rewards of this learning and improving practice have more than offset the difficulties and risks involved in research. Indeed, we have seen the use of the FAF transform the cultures of other agencies, and we invite you to experiment with it in your own work.

The entire introduction is important to read in order to gain a comprehensive understanding of the FAF including its history, development, format, design, and directions as to how to use it as a practice and evaluation instrument. Specifically, agencies or program administrators considering using the FAF should read it in its entirety. Once the decision is made to use the FAF, specific sections are more designed for certain user groups based on their roles and interests.

---

* The authors acknowledge the staff members and families of Children's Bureau of Southern California for their assistance and input on this introduction and instruction guide.

This version of the FAF is based on the wisdom and experience of many parents, practitioners, supervisors, and administrators. Without their participation, development of the FAF would not have been possible. The authors would also like to thank Judy Nelson (the previous executive director of Children's Bureau) for her leadership in initiating this effort, and Alex Morales (the current executive director) for his commitment and continuing support.

Two of the authors of this monograph (McCroskey and Sladen) have been involved with the development of the FAF since the beginning; the third (Meezan) has taken major responsibility for its development as a research instrument. We have very different perspectives and ways of approaching tasks, different expectations and standards for success, and different experiences with the FAF—and it has been our ability to share these differences, among ourselves and with the many others who have contributed to its development, that has made this experience so rewarding. We invite additional input and suggestions for improving the form, as well as information about its use in different settings. Please address correspondence to: Family Assessment Form, Children's Bureau of Southern California, 3910 Oakwood Avenue, Los Angeles, CA 90004.

WHY FAMILY ASSESSMENT?

The primary challenge of delivering and evaluating family-based services is in successfully assessing changes in *families* rather than in the *individuals* who are the recipients of service. While other programs, both within and outside the field of child welfare, focus their evaluations on changes in individuals, family-based services have as their major goal changing the transactions among family members, no matter how inclusive or limited the definition of the family might be. It is thus necessary, for both clinical and evaluation purposes, for the field to develop measures that go beyond traditional assessments of risks to the safety and well-being of children, the capacities and attitudes of parents, or the mental health status of individual family members (important though all of these may be). We need measures that enable practitioners to capture family circumstances and the complex transactions among family members.

Assessment is clearly a key concept in service delivery. In order to help, the worker first needs to understand what is going on within the family and its ecology now as well as what may have gone on in the past. While people trained in different professions may use the term somewhat differently (e.g., doctors assess symptoms in order to make a diagnosis, intake workers assess the need for and appropriateness of the specific services that are available, teachers assess how much of what is known to determine what needs to be taught), assessment is widely acknowledged to be the key to effective service planning in any kind of social, educational or health service. If it is often difficult to thoroughly, accurately and sensitively assess the situation of an individual who comes for service; these difficulties are multiplied when a worker—especially one who is likely to be rushed, stressed, and overburdened—tries to assess an entire family. Assessment of a family at intake is also critical for research purposes. If one does not know what a family "looked like" when they entered service, how can one possibly know if they changed during the course of service? Without baseline data, how can one measure progress?

There may not be one correct assessment instrument that will fit all family-based service programs since family attributes and cultures, agency settings, and program goals vary. It is clear, however, that all family-based programs need measures and methods of measuring that are valid and reliable, culturally sensitive, and strengths-oriented. Practitioners must be involved in the process of developing such instruments, since workers have the best sense of the information available to them and experience with the ways that families respond to different kinds of questions and assessment procedures. Further, if workers are involved in design of their assessment instruments, and if these instruments reflect sensitivity to clinical practice, other practitioners will be more likely to see these procedures as useful, and it will be easier to engage them in collecting and recording assessment information.

DEVELOPMENT OF THE FAMILY ASSESSMENT FORM: A CASE HISTORY

Children's Bureau of Southern California (CBSC) began its in-home family-based services program—the Family Connection Program—in 1983. An assessment completed shortly thereafter highlighted four pressing program needs: the need to collect standardized information on all families; the need for a more thorough initial family assessment to facilitate effective service planning; the need for ongoing staff training; and the need for a greater understanding of the range of possible client outcomes.

During discussions with staff members after this initial program assessment, the agency's research consultant asked: "What do you want to know about the work you do?" There was substantial agreement among staff that the definitions of success for this program should go well beyond placement avoidance, and staff recognized that systematic assessment of multiple factors impacting their client families would be essential if changes in family functioning were to be captured and documented.

A committee was formed that included direct service staff members, the program director, the consulting psychologist, the research consultant, and agency administrators. Their task was to attempt to define operationally the complex idea of family functioning as it pertained to this specific program. This committee reviewed a set of data collection instruments used by similar programs as well at those reported in the literature. Unfortunately, none matched the needs of the program at that time. It was therefore decided to build an instrument specific to the needs of the program, guided, in part, by aspects of available instruments. All agreed that this instrument was to be based on practitioner judgment about the information they felt was essential in assessing families in this home-based services program. Continuing discussions about what the program was trying to accomplish, and how it could best do so, helped both to unite staff from different service locations into an effective team and bond agency administrators and consultants to the clinicians . Workers originated or approved each item, developed a guide, and participated in ongoing discussions regarding revisions and modifications of the form. Reciprocally, administrators and consultants went on in-home visits with practitioners to try to understand the realities of the using the FAF with families in their homes. While the final product had some similarities to other instruments that were developed at the same time [Magura & Moses 1986; Magura et al. 1987], its unique qualities derive from the fact that it was designed by practitioners to meet their needs.

Since being made available to other agencies in 1988–89, the FAF has been used in family preservation, family support, reunification, adoption, maternal and child health, early intervention, and head start programs (among those known). Workers in these settings have reported that, when used well, the FAF can be extremely helpful for clinical practice. In their view, the fact that it is also useful for program evaluation purposes is an important, but secondary, benefit.

The version of the FAF presented here is the tangible result of an ongoing, interactive, iterative, process among practitioners, administrators, consultants, researchers, and numerous people outside of CBSC, all of whom have become engaged by a number of questions critical to good clinical practice with families: How do we assess functioning when families come for service? How do we use this information to help? How do we know what we and they have achieved by the time they leave? What is "adequate" family functioning and how much progress is "enough"?

DESCRIPTION OF THE FAMILY ASSESSMENT FORM

While the FAF was developed to meet the needs of all practitioners, it was intended to be especially useful for those at the bachelor's level or those with little exposure to systematic assessment procedures. It is especially useful in home-based services, as it helps workers who leave the known and comfortable world of the office to structure client assessment in the infinitely more complex atmosphere of family homes and communities.

The FAF has four key characteristics that distinguish it from others currently used in the field.

1. The FAF is first and foremost a practice instrument, developed by and responsive to the needs of practitioners.

2. It defines and measures family functioning from an ecological perspective, assessing context as well as transactions among family members and their environments.

3. It documents family strengths as well as problems and concerns, supporting practice approaches that recognize and build upon a family's strengths and potential for resilience.

4. It is designed to serve multiple purposes in an agency setting, and has a demonstrated potential to integrate family assessment, service planning, case documentation, and program evaluation.

The FAF helps workers to assess families at the beginning of service, to develop individualized family service plans, to monitor family progress, and to assess outcomes for individual families. Since it is standardized, the FAF also allows programs or agencies to look at their overall effectiveness by aggregating the data gathered about individual families. CBSC's experience with the FAF as a practice/research tool has confirmed the belief that the timely accurate assessment of family functioning, linked to the development of a service plan, can not only strengthen service for families but, over time, can produce helpful information about program effectiveness and the kinds of families who benefit most from services.

The FAF collects information on the family's environment, the caregivers, the children, and transactions among family members. Strengths and concerns noted on the form become the basis of service planning with the family. The form includes a Face Sheet (noting names, referral information, presenting problems, etc.), a Behavioral Concerns/Observation Checklist for all children in the home, a Service Plan, and a Closing Summary. The FAF also assesses history and personal characteristics of caregivers (areas which are not expected to change as a result of this service) and six areas of family functioning which may change as a result of the intervention. These six areas may be used to measure family functioning in programs that approach intervention from a variety of theoretical perspectives as long as they are anticipating effects in any or all of these family functioning areas.

The following are the six areas of family functioning:

- living conditions;
- financial conditions;
- interactions between the adult caregivers;
- interactions between caregivers and children;
- support available to the family; and
- developmental stimulation available to children.

Items on the FAF are designed to be rated on a nine point scale (1, 1.5, 2, 2.5, etc.) in relation to family strengths and severity of problems. Individual items are rated on a nine point scale. A rating of 1 represents unusual strength while a rating of 5 represents severe problems that may endanger a child's health and safety, threaten a caregiver's well-being, indicate severely dysfunctional family interactions, or call for removal of children from the family home. Workers are also given the option to rate at the midway point between two numbers (i.e., 2.5 is between a 2 and a 3). The overall meaning of ratings are listed on page xxiv.

Practitioners have also developed detailed *operational definitions*, or examples, of the observations, behavior, or responses that would lead them to assign a particular rating. These "keys" to rating are incorporated on the instrument as anchors to increase objectivity and consistency of ratings. However, other situations not included may fall within a given severity rating.

The FAF ratings direct attention to both strengths and areas of concern. Re-ratings at termination and/or later follow-up periods measure changes in family functioning during and after the service period. Thus, the FAF enables workers to conduct a complete psychosocial assessment that is recorded in a quantitative manner and allows them to monitor progress with a family.

MAKING THE FAF WORK FOR YOU:
TRAINING, SUPERVISION, AND SUPPORT

Administrators or managers who are considering use of the FAF should recognize that practitioners will need training and support in incorporating the FAF into their practice. Because the "buy-in" of practitioners is absolutely essential for the effectiveness of a practice-based instrument such as the FAF, preparation for its use should include discussions between various levels of agency or program administration and line staff members about whether this approach is appropriate to the specific agency setting and how it might be made more appropriate. Administrators and workers must decide whether the FAF "fits" with the program's basic approach to practice—if it does not fit well with the program's theory base, the values and beliefs of practitioners, or the structure of the program, it may be perceived as just another administrative requirement, with little chance of successful incorporation into daily practice.

Managers should ensure that a process through which staff input is sought and incorporated is developed. Such a process should include discussions of the form's relevance to program purposes and current practice methods; changes that might be needed to make it more useful; current paperwork that could be changed or diminished if the form were adopted; procedures for tracking and using the FAF; training needed to support practitioners in their transition to using the form; and ongoing discussions about the form's usefulness and procedural and substantive modifications which would be helpful. In addition, during these discussions, items can be deleted, added, reorganized, or altered to the FAF to fit clinical, procedural, and/or program needs. Again, we suggest that the six key areas of family functioning be left intact and used individually or as a set.

The version of the FAF presented is designed to allow individualized consideration of each of the three FAF modules: *outcome ratings*—the six factors of family functioning which may change as a result of services; *constant items*—ratings of caregiver history and personal characteristics which are necessary for a complete psychosocial assessment but which may not change as a result of services; and *operational elements* of the form including intake and referral information, the child behavior checklist, and the service planning and closing forms. Some users may decide to use only the outcome items—all six factors or fewer—while others may want to use the entire form.

The use of the FAF does not demand that an agency duplicate information they already collect in another form. However, if current agency forms are maintained, efforts should be made to assure that information from various sources is consistent in terms of definitions and assumptions. Data management and analysis procedures should also be designed to allow for cross-referencing between data bases so that analysts do not miss the opportunity to try to account for changes in outcome variables based on information collected on other forms. For example, if demographic information is not collected on the FAF, and the multiple agency data bases do not "speak" to each other, there will be no way to relate these variables to case progress.

When the decision has been made to use the FAF, managers will need to set up training sessions to familiarize workers with the form and its use. At CBSC, this normally takes two half day sessions, about one month apart, which allows sufficient time for workers to practice using the FAF between training sessions. CBSC staff are available to answer training questions or to consult on designing the most effective training sessions. Contact CBSC at 1–888/ALL–4–KIDS or at their web site address, www.all4kids.org.

The first training session includes three parts and a homework assignment.

An Introduction during which the trainer discusses the background and history of the development of the form and the rationale for its use in the program or agency.

"A Walk Through the FAF" during which workers are guided through their own copies of the form by the trainer, who describes each section of the form and its individual items. Throughout this portion of the training, the trainer should focus on items that may not be self-evident, and workers should be encouraged to ask questions and to discuss the meaning, importance, and intent of the individual items.

A "Hands On" exercise which occurs after the form has been discussed and initial questions are answered. Workers should be instructed to think of a family that they know well and to complete one section of the form. This exercise generally raises more questions, as people debrief and compare their experiences, the knowledge they had to bring to bear to be able to rate items, and their uncertainties about how to apply the rating scheme to an individual family and their circumstances.

Homework: At the end of the session, workers should be instructed to use the form with at least one family during the next month and to be prepared to discuss their experiences at the next session.

The second training session usually includes six topics and another homework assignment.

Responses to Using the FAF during which the trainer asks people to recount their experiences in using the FAF for the first time. The trainer should expect that these initial experiences will vary among workers—some may state "It is too long and I couldn't do it," while others will claim to have "completed it easily." The trainer should strive to normalize the frustration that comes with learning to do something new, and to help people recognize that they are beginning a process that will take some time before it becomes second nature. (Experience at CBSC suggests that workers who are comfortable and experienced with the FAF can complete it in about 1 to 1.5 hours.)

"A Second Walk Through the FAF" during which the trainer should elicit responses on items from the whole group, illustrating the range or unanimity of opinion on how to rate each item. Trainers should expect that the group will have very different opinions on some items and that many of these differences will be based on culture or basic values about how families should live. The trainer should try to bring these differences to the surface for discussion, rather than covering them over in generalities. It is important to know how and why workers may vary in their ratings.

Discussion of the Service Plan and Goal Setting during which the trainer talks about working with families to set appropriate goals based on both strengths and concerns. The trainer may also ask workers for examples of the FAF Service Plan completed during the last month to help illustrate how to use item ratings to think about *problems*, set *goals*, and devise *methods* to meet those goals. For many practitioners, this is the most challenging part of the FAF.

Discussion of "Judging" Families during which the trainer should ask workers about their reactions to rating families. For some workers, rating feels uncomfortably like "judging." Workers may be hesitant to judge negatively when they feel that parents are "good people" who are trying hard in a difficult situation or facing difficult circumstances. Thus, initial low FAF ratings may raise the question, "If these families don't have problems, why are they at our agency?" The trainer should stress that FAF ratings are a "snapshot" of a family at a point in time, a point when they are coming for help, rather than a judgment of their potential for improvement.

Discussion of Working with and Building on Family Strengths during which the trainer should also stress that "strengths" (ratings of 1 or 2) are also important because they suggest *how* to best work with families to achieve goals. Recent research shows that resilience is perhaps more common than had been previously thought even among the most disadvantaged families and their children [Anthony & Cohler 1987; Werner & Smith 1992; Schweinhart, Barnes & Weikart 1993]. The FAF rating and summary process facilitates identification of client strengths from which to build problem-solving and coping skills, and helps workers identify, acknowledge, and enumerate these strengths in their discussions with families.

Next Steps during which ideas about adjusting the form to better meet the needs of the individual program and its workers and information-handling procedures may rise. Topics for future training such as how to assess substance abuse or ask about past experiences of child abuse may also form. Workers should be asked how they would like to proceed, including scheduling more training, beginning regular use of the FAF with some or all of their clients, using the FAF in supervision, etc.

Homework: Unless there are unresolved problems with its use, workers should be asked to begin regular use of the FAF (perhaps only with new families or only for a specific part of their caseloads), to be prepared to bring a completed FAF to their next individual or group supervision session, and to use it regularly in supervision. In addition, managers or supervisors may want to use the FAF as the basis for team case conferences.

Ongoing support should be built into the regular staff development and supervision processes of the agency. Perhaps the most effective approach is to use the FAF regularly during supervision and periodically during team meetings to discuss and clarify ratings and discuss service planning and delivery issues. While consistency of ratings among workers is the ultimate goal, it is most helpful initially to ask for a variety of opinions and to stimulate discussion about why people see things differently. Full discussion of why two workers see the same behavior differently often reveals unexplored and helpful differences in perception, values, and beliefs among workers.

It is also helpful to discuss certain FAF items with families, exploring areas in which worker judgment may be very different from those of family members. Such discussions can take place during the assessment rating period or prior to service planning. Differences in perceptions between worker and caregivers should be expected in many areas, since they tend to see things from different, but equally valid, vantage points. Understanding these differences of perception will be extremely useful to both parties during the process of working together.

The FAF allows differences between the values and beliefs of workers and families to be identified and discussed sensitively. When the culture or socioeconomic class of the practitioner is different from that of the family, assumptions and values about how families should work, how parents should behave, and how children should act, may be at odds with each other. Although it is clear that assessment should be sensitive to cultural and class assumptions and values, it is often not clear how to operationalize that sensitivity. One of the reasons that FAF was designed as a rating device rather than as a questionnaire was that this format allows for differences in perception between families and workers to emerge. The emergence of these differences, when they do occur, allows workers to discuss and teach expected behavioral standards and the universals of child development while, at the same time, it allows families to teach workers about the meanings of behavior within their cultural group and community context.

Since the form does not dictate the order in which items are completed, the way to discuss them with the family, or the cultural context for their interpretation, it leaves issues of cultural sensitivity to the worker and supervisor. When the FAF is used by culturally sensitive workers, who allow discussion of these issues to emerge with the family, the assessment and service plan will be sensitive; when workers are not sensitive to the nuances of culture, class or values, due either to poor training or personal biases, ratings will not be culturally sensitive.

USING THE FAF FOR PROGRAM EVALUATION

CBSC has utilized the FAF as a program evaluation tool for some years, using both overall goal achievement and changes between pre- and post-test scores on specific items or scales as primary indicators of success. This is relatively easy for any agency to do, requiring only that forms are complete, data entry is managed systematically, and a simple statistical analysis software package is available.

Following the acceptance of the FAF as a clinical tool at CBSC, researchers began to assess its reliability and validity. After some experience with evaluation using the FAF, the agency was willing to take a bigger risk, and helped to initiate a study in Los Angeles using a rigorous experimental design which also provided important information about the FAF itself [Meezan & McCroskey 1996; McCroskey & Meezan 1997]. Other studies have also provided very helpful information [Amland 1996; Meezan & O'Keefe, under review].

This section gives a brief synopsis of knowledge about the reliability and validity of FAF to date. It contains some technical information that may be of more interest to researchers than to practitioners. However, such information may be helpful to agency-based researchers who need to determine the potential research applications of the FAF in each individual agency setting. Additional information will be available in a forthcoming article [Meezan & McCroskey, in preparation]. (For more information, contact William Meezan or Jacquelyn McCroskey at the University of Southern California School of Social Work, Montgomery Ross Fisher Building, Los Angeles, CA 90089–0411.)

Inter-Rater Reliability

Inter-rater reliability for the individual items which appear on the FAF has been assessed for both clinical judgements and research purposes. Clinically, teams of workers at CBSC (and in other agencies) have rated the same families independently and compared their scores. Depending on the situation, ratings have been the same or within one-half step of each other about 75-80% of the time. Such trials, in which workers rate independently, can be used for training purposes; they can also provide information useful to supervisors and administrators on the comparability of rating styles across workers.

In terms of more formal research, the FAF has been adapted to a research interview format [Meezan & McCroskey 1996; McCroskey & Meezan in press]. Research interviews were tape-recorded which allowed for assessment of inter-rater reliability. Double coding of these interviews, based on audio tapes, was completed for a 10% sample of the families at intake, which produced a total of 970 comparisons. Reliability between the two raters was as follows: exact correspondence = 50%; +/- a half step in rating = 73.5%; +/- a full step in rating = 89.2%. These inter-rater reliabilities are clearly acceptable given the fact that audio tapes were used rather than double observation during the interviews. (For a copy of the research interview, contact either Dr. Jacquelyn McCroskey or Dr. William Meezan at the address above.)

Construct Validity Based on Factor Analysis

The first factor analysis of the FAF research interview, based on 240 cases in the Los Angeles study, yielded an interpretable six factor solution which explained 63% of the variance. Other analyses, based on worker observation and ratings of these same cases, yielded a similar solution. Some FAF items were not included in these analysis since they were either not applicable to all cases (presence of pre-school and school-aged children and their peer interactions), they were independent rather than dependent variables (family history or personality characteristics), or they did not load appropriately high on any one factor. No item loaded higher on another factor than on the one in which it was placed, and all factor loadings were above .4. The factors, and the items and their loadings associated with them, which were derived and named by Meezan and McCroskey [in preparation], are displayed in table 1.

TABLE 1
Six-Factor Solution of FAF Items Based on Researcher Interviewer

Factor and Items	Item Loading	Alpha	Variance Explained Rotated Component	% Total Variance Explained
Parent-Child Interactions		.90	7.0	18.36
Consistent Discipline	.84			
Appropriate Discipline	.83			
Child Development	.77			
Attitude toward Parenting	.75			
Bonding with Child	.75			
Child Communication with Caregiver	.73			
Bonding with Caregiver	.70			
Use of Physical Discipline	.68			
Caregiver Communication with Child	.65			
Takes Appropriate Authority Role	.58			
Child Cooperation with Caregiver	.51			
Schedule for Children	.48			
Living Conditions		.76	3.24	8.53
Outside Safety	.86			
Outside Cleanliness	.86			
Inside Safety	.63			
Inside Cleanliness	.58			
Outside Play	.45			
Caregiver Interactions		.92	4.73	12.44
Intercommunication	.88			
Supportive Relationships	.88			
Attitude toward Each Other	.84			
Conjoint Problem-Solving	.80			
Conflict	.79			
Power	.76			
Supports for Parents		.76	3.12	8.20
Maintains Adult Relationships	.73			
Child Care	.72			
Friend Support	.66			
Chooses Appropriate Substitutes	.53			
Medical Care	.52			
Family Support	.49			
Financial Conditions		.71	3.16	8.30
Financial Management	.74			
Stress due to Welfare	.68			
Inside Furniture	.62			
Financial Stress	.57			
Transportation	.53			
Developmental Stimulation		.76	2.32	6.10
Appropriate Toys	.67			
Learning Experiences	.58			
Time for Play	.53			
Sibling Interactions	.42			

Inter-Item Reliability of Scales

After deriving subscales based on the factor analyses, inter-item reliability (Chronbach's Alpha) were derived. Two items were dropped in order to raise alpha. Internal consistency for these final subscales was quite good for both the worker observational form and the researcher completed interview versions of the FAF, ranging from .68 to .93. These scores are reported in table 2. Other studies, using the FAF interview form, have shown very similar alpha coefficients for these scales [Meezan & O'Keefe, in press].

TABLE 2
Internal Consistency Data on Six-Factor Solution Based on Interviewer and Worker Supplied Information

	Interviewer Alpha	Worker Alpha
Parent-Child Interactions	.90	.93
Living Conditions	.76	.87
Caregiver Interactions	.92	.88
Supports for Parents	.76	.72
Financial Conditions	.71	.78
Developmental Stimulation	.76	.69

A PRACTITIONER'S GUIDE TO USING THE FAMILY ASSESSMENT FORM

The Family Assessment Form (FAF) gives practitioners a structured way to document an assessment of family functioning. While it has been used as a structured interview for formal research inquiries, it was designed as an observational guide and a framework for psychosocial assessment of families. Used as a framework for assessment, the FAF allows workers time to develop a relationship with the family, to introduce questions when they are appropriate and natural, and to use their own judgments about how best to approach sensitive items. The FAF thus supplements the worker's natural style and approach, rather than driving the pacing or flow of initial interviews. It provides a structure for thinking about and observing families, and should not interfere with the development of a trusting relationship or meeting the immediate needs of families or children.

Ratings are based on observation, reports by family members and others involved, and the worker's own clinical judgments. Once the information is gathered, the worker should have a good picture of the family and its individual strengths, concerns and risk areas. In some cases, the worker may also want to ask family members to rate their own situations, so that the two ratings can be compared and discussed. The worker and family together should set concrete and focused goals for an agreed upon service period. At CBSC, workers rate FAF items after each visit, and usually take up to four visits to complete the entire form, including the service plan. Completion of the FAF after each session with the family also points to additional areas on which to focus future interviews and observations.

At the end of the service period, the worker rates the family again on a new copy of the form. Using a new form minimizes the possibility that closing ratings will be overly influenced by initial ratings. Comparison of the initial and termination ratings provides data on changes during the service period. Workers and families can also evaluate progress and plan for the future.

Completing the FAF Face Sheet

Fill in the *case number, worker name,* and *program/office* on the lines at the top of the page. Indicate with an **X** whether this is the *Time 1* (assessment) or *Time 2* (termination) rating in the boxes provided. *Persons assessed* should only include those people directly involved in the service. To maintain confidentiality, use only the first names of family members and provide their *relationship* to others in the family. Children should be listed from youngest to oldest. Indicate *age* rather than date of birth for easy reference, and note *others in home* and their *relationship* to the family. (*Relationship* is meant to indicate the complexity of the family, such as parent, stepchild, grandparent, friend of Caregiver A, etc. This can be left blank if desired or found to be irrelevant for your purposes.)

Presenting problem refers to the actual incident(s) (alleged, substantiated or denied) which brought the family to the agency. Choose the problem for which the family was referred, even if the family does not view this as their most pressing problem. Specify who the family was referred by and why the referral was made. Use one of the *Presenting Problem Codes* which, in your opinion, best captures the most severe presenting problem at time of case referral (the list of codes appears on page xxiii.)

Child protective services involvement refers to the chronicity of problems which may affect the prognosis for the case. This information may need to be verified or obtained from the public child protective services agency (CPS). Write N/A if the family was not referred by CPS.

Out-of-home placement(s) refers to any time the child(ren) have lived away from the primary caregiver(s), whether in kinship care, family foster care, mental health facilities, or other institutional settings. Do not include short, planned visits or absences from home. The occurrence of past or current out-of-home care is related to the prognosis for outcome and the risk for future placement. Circle "yes" or "no" after each question. This information may need to be verified or obtained from CPS. Be sure to enter the first names of children placed. Comments may be used to clarify the information which has been recorded.

Medical/psychiatric involvement refers to significant or chronic medical problems in the family and/or a history of mental illness, counseling, therapy, or hospitalization. Circle "yes" or "no." Comments should be used to clarify and elaborate on the information presented.

Dates of the *initial assessment* reflect the dates and length of time spent with the family to collect information necessary to complete the FAF. Depending on circumstances, up to three interviews may be needed to complete the assessment. It is important that initial assessment ratings take place within this time frame so as to establish a baseline for later ratings. Indicate whether or not the information was gathered in the family's home. Comments should be used to clarify the information recorded.

Rating the FAF Family Functioning Factors

For the initial assessment circle the numbered rating to the right of the item which best reflects the family's situation at the opening of the case. Use the operational definitions of ratings 1, 2, 3, 4 and 5 at the right of each item to help anchor each rating. Operational definitions include tangible manifestations that may be seen, heard, or discussed with family members. Use the half point (1.5, 2.5, 3.5, 4.5) to indicate when ratings appear to fall between the operational definitions listed. Items rated 3 or more indicate problems or possible areas to target in terms of service goals. Items rated 2.5 or less reflect areas in which there are no immediate problems or where there are family strengths.

The specifics used in the operational definitions are meant as examples only. Using a given numeric rating does not mean that all listed conditions exist or that one of the exact conditions listed is present. Consider the age of child, the family's cultural context, and other pertinent factors to determine the rating. When the operational definitions do not specifically reflect the family's situation, use the overall meaning of scores, located on page xxiv, to help select a rating. It is important to rate each item. Make the best clinical judgment possible with the information available.

Some items require two scores if there are multiple caregivers or for other reasons as noted on the form. Caregiver A should always be the mother, if there is a mother involved in the case. Be sure to be consistent, always referring to the same persons as caregiver A and B. Some items may not apply to some families. Use N/A to indicate that the information is not applicable in this case. Strengths and concerns in each area should be noted, in the space provided, to clarify and specify items as needed.

Rating Caregiver History and Characteristics on the FAF

Items in this section are generally not expected to change as a result of home-based services. These items are rated at the point of initial assessment to provide background information about the family and to suggest issues that may be important in service planning and delivery.

Sometimes caregivers are reluctant to talk about sensitive items (such as sexual abuse or substance use) with a new worker. If more is learned about the caregiver or the family as the case progresses, update these items at termination to reflect your new knowledge about the family. These items are not used to measure program outcomes rather to help describe the characteristics of families that benefit and those that do not. The individual items in this section are rated in the same manner as that discussed in the previous section.

Completing the FAF Behavioral Concerns/Observation Checklist

The purpose of this section is to facilitate the identification of behavior problems or concerns for individual children from the perspective of the caregivers, worker or others. In the left-hand column check any of the listed behaviors that apply to any child in the family. Check "staff" if the behavior is exhibited in your presence or is reported by another professional; check "caregiver" if the behavior is reported by a caregiver. Note the first name of the child exhibiting the behavior and the frequency of its occurrence. If a child exhibits more than one of the behaviors listed, circle all those that apply.

You may want to have the checklist with you as you observe the family and talk with the caregivers. If you choose to do this, ask, in a general sense, about any concerns the caregiver has with a child's behavior. If many behavior concerns are reported note them on the form. If the caregivers express no particular concerns, ask whether the child's teachers or other people have reported any problems. Take a moment with the caregivers to highlight the major behavioral categories on the form to see if the caregiver thinks there is a problem (e.g., "Does John have any eating or sleeping difficulties?", "What kind of grades does Marie get in school?", "Is Tommy potty trained?").

Most of the problems listed are self explanatory. A brief description of each item is listed along with suggestions for detailing the problem. Additional questions about the nature of the behavior may help in formulating an intervention plan. These additional questions may include when the behavior occurs, how often it occurs, under what circumstances it occurs, what modifies the behavior, what makes it better or worse or more or less frequent, when it started and who is most concerned.

Completing the FAF Service Plan

The FAF service plan should be developed jointly with the family using the ratings and comments noted on the FAF to identify key family strengths and problems. Three types of information are recorded on the service plan: family or child *problems*/concerns, service *goals*, and *methods*.

Review the FAF for those areas rated 3 or more (i.e., 3, 3.5, 4, 4.5, 5) and talk with the family to decide which are the most appropriate and important to work on at this time. Note that some areas which are assessed will not be appropriate for intervention (because they are not expected to change, the family does not see them as important, or they fall outside of the worker's focus, capacity or resources). Other items give information on how to work most effectively with specific families. For example, "learning ability/style" helps the worker determine how best to present new information. Identify those problem areas on which you and the family agree to work. List these and indicate the rating (1 to 5) assigned to this area at the point of initial assessment. A grey box is provided on the Service Plan to record the rating and the FAF item number.

For each problem area, identify the *goal* and method you plan to use to address this problem. For example, if you have selected caregiver "takes appropriate authority role with children" as an important presenting problem, identify the specific goal which might most fit the needs of this caregiver. For one family, the goal may be "to increase the parents' ability to use authority in setting expectations for the older children, especially in terms of completing chores." For another family, the goal might be "to decrease the caregiver's demands on John and help her to allow him independent action in his use of play time." The specifics should be phrased in terms of the needs and characteristics of the particular family at this point in time.

The *methods* specified should be those which can best help this family given its specific strengths and concerns. For example, methods of helping caregivers deal with authority issues might be attendance at parent education classes, the use of modeling techniques with the caregivers and child, or discussion of reading materials about parental authority and age-appropriate expectations. Identify the methods that seem most appropriate for the family. The examples provided in table 3 may spark your thinking about problems, goals, and methods and might help workers who are new to the FAF think about the linkages between them.

Note at the bottom of the page the estimated duration of service, e.g., 3 months, and the estimated frequency of contact, e.g., 2 times a week, that will be required to complete this service plan. If you want to add or change a goal or methods, use an extra form to indicate this new information. Keep the original form and all subsequent additions in the case file.

Completing the FAF Closing Summary

The closing summary is used to detail and evaluate the progress made by the family. Before completing this section, workers should first complete their termination ratings of the individual FAF items. To do this, workers use a new FAF and complete the ratings as they did initially. For the termination rating, it is not necessary to complete the entire face sheet again. Workers need only note the *case #*, *worker's name*, and **X** the *Time 2* box at the top of the face sheet.

At the top of the closing summary form, workers should note the *case #, worker's name, program/office*, and *dates* of case opening and closing. Workers should check the *reason* for closing: Did the family complete the program, move, refuse service, or drop out of service? Did the worker decide to terminate the case ahead of the projected termination date? Was there another reason for case closure at this time?

Under *outcome on goals*, indicate in narrative form observable changes related to the problems selected for attention in the family's service plan. Indicate the ratings you assigned to each targeted problem area at initial assessment and at termination. If a problem area has been changed or dropped during the course of the case, put N/A in the second rating space. If additional goals were added, use an additional sheet to record assessment and termination ratings.

TABLE 3
Examples of Possible Answers to the Service Plan Portion of the Family Assessment Form

Possible Problem Area	Possible Goals	Possible Methods
safety outside home maintenance	remove outside safety hazards; have parents contact landlord to improve safety	work with caregivers and landlord to remove/repair hazards
extended family or friend support	to improve relationships with specific family members	support in contacting specific friends or family; moderate joint discussion between caregiver and family members or friends
discipline	to reduce use of physical discipline; to expand range of disciplinary techniques; to increase use of positive reinforcement	reading and discussion on appropriate disciplining techniques; guide caregiver's experimentation with appropriate techniques; monitor and encourage consistency in use of discipline

Under *summary of progress*, indicate whether you feel that progress was made in this case. Check "yes" or "no" to indicate overall progress, and then comment on the amount and kind of progress made. This may be different than the ratings for specific problem areas. For example, progress could have been made in areas other than those you originally selected for attention, thus making your summary more positive than the specific ratings would indicate. Or things may have deteriorated in areas that need further explanation than the rating alone.

Under *family's summary of progress*, indicate what the family thinks about their progress. Base this on specific discussions with the family.

Under *disposition/referral* indicate whether any of the children left the home for any type of out-of-home placement since the beginning of the case. Specify whether it was in kinship care, in family foster care, in institutional care, or in some other out-of-home care arrangement.

Under *service referrals* indicate all services to which the family was referred during the service period or at termination. Indicate whether the family received services, if known.

Under *comments* make any additional comments that would help someone else reading the FAF (e.g., supervisor, administrator, or evaluator) understand progress in this case or any special conditions that affected progress.

REFERENCES

Amland, R. (1996). Family preservation: The impact of poverty, environment and family characteristics on family functioning (unpublished Ph.D. dissertation, University of Southern California, School of Public Administration).

Anthony, E. J., & Cohler, B. (1987). *The invulnerable child.* New York: The Guilford Press.

Magura, S., & Moses, B. (1986). *Outcome measures for child welfare services: Theory and applications.* Washington, DC: Child Welfare League of America.

Magura, S., Moses, B., & Jones, M. A. (1987). *Assessing risk and measuring change in families: The Family Risk Scales.* Washington, DC: Child Welfare League of America.

McCroskey, J., & Nelson, J. (1989). Practice-based research in a family support program: The Family Connection Project Example. *Child Welfare, 68,* 573–587.

McCroskey, J., Nishimoto, R., & Subramanian, K. (1991). Assessment in family support programs: Initial reliability and validity testing of the Family Assessment Form. *Child Welfare, 70,* 19–33.

McCroskey, J., & Meezan, W. (1997). *Family preservation and family functioning.* Washington, DC: Child Welfare League of America.

Meezan, W., & McCroskey, J. (1996, Winter). Improving family functioning through family preservation services: Results of the Los Angeles Experiment. *Family Preservation Journal,* 9–29.

Meezan, W., & McCroskey, J. (in preparation). The Family Assessment Form: Further information on its reliability and validity (expected submission to *Social Work Research*).

Meezan, W., & O'Keefe, M. (under review). Multi-family group therapy: Impact on family functioning and child behavior. *Child Welfare.*

Pecora, P., Fraser, M., Nelson, K., McCroskey, J., & Meezan, W. (1995). *Evaluating family based services.* Hawthorne, NY: Aldine de Gruyter.

Schweinhart, L., Barnes, H. & Weikart, D. (1993). *Significant benefits: The High/Scope Perry Preschool Study through age 27.* Ypsilanti, MI: High/Scope Press.

Werner, E., & Smith, R. (1992). *Overcoming the odds: High risk children from birth to adulthood.* Ithaca, NY: Cornell University Press.

Presenting Problem Codes

Select one of the following which best summarizes the major presenting problem, the problem of greatest severity known, at case referral.

1 Child sexual abuse

2 Child physical abuse

3 Child emotional abuse

4 Family violence which may result in child abuse

5 Child neglect

6 Caregiver feels unable to cope with child(ren)

7 Difficult child behavior

8 Caregiver disability or illness

9 School problems

10 At-risk new or first-time parent/birth

11 Other child/family problems

Overall Meaning of Scores

Consider the age of child, the family's cultural context, and other pertinent factors to determine the rating. When the operational definitions do not specifically reflect the family's situation, use the overall meaning of scores to help select a rating. It is important to rate each item. Make the best clinical judgment possible with the information available.

1   Above average in this area. There are positive influences or traits that have a strengthening effect on the family and/or child(ren).

2   Generally adequate. Minor problems are within normal limits; they are not necessarily nonexistent, but do not create problems for caregiver(s) or child(ren). Problem of such a minor nature that treatment or intervention is not necessary, but may be desired by caregivers to improve parenting.

3   Problems of a moderate nature. Problems of a moderate degree have a negative impact on the welfare of children or put the family at risk. Treatment or counseling or parent training are indicated.

4   Problems of a major nature. These have a significant negative influence on children or caregiver's well-being. Intervention is required; chronicity needs to be considered.

5   Situation endangering to children's health, safety, and well-being. This degree of problem may call for removal of children temporarily or permanently, or prevent return of children to family home. Situation requires intervention and monitoring; chronicity must be assessed.

Face Sheet

Face Sheet

CASE # _____   WORKER _____   PROGRAM/OFFICE _____

Persons Assessed*	Age	Relationship
Caregiver A _____	_____	_____
Caregiver B _____	_____	_____
Child 1 _____	_____	_____
Child 2 _____	_____	_____
Child 3 _____	_____	_____
Child 4 _____	_____	_____
Child 5 _____	_____	_____
Child 6 _____	_____	_____
Child 7 _____	_____	_____
Child 8 _____	_____	_____

Others in Home	Age	Relationship
_____	_____	_____
_____	_____	_____
_____	_____	_____
_____	_____	_____

* NOTE: List children from youngest to oldest.

PRESENTING PROBLEMS(S): Code # _____ Referred by: _____

For what reason: _____

_____

_____

_____

CHILD PROTECTIVE SERVICES INVOLVEMENT

Number of past involvements with CPS_____

Length of current involvement with CPS _____

OUT-OF-HOME PLACEMENT(S)	CIRCLE	NAME(S)
Past out-of-home placement(s)?	YES/NO	Child(ren) _____
Current out-of-home placement(s)?	YES/NO	Child(ren) _____
At risk of out-of-home placement(s)?	YES/NO	Child(ren) _____

Comments: _____

_____

_____

MEDICAL/PSYCHIATRIC INVOLVEMENT	CIRCLE AND EXPLAIN
Significant or chronic medical problems?	YES/NO _____
Contact with mental health system/professionals?	YES/NO _____

Comments: _____

_____

_____

Initial Assessment

In-Home

Dates_____ Hours _____   Yes/No

Dates_____ Hours _____   Yes/No

Dates_____ Hours _____   Yes/No

Comments: _____

_____

_____

_____

Family Functioning Factors

Sections A through F

SECTION A: LIVING CONDITIONS*

A1. Cleanliness/Orderliness—Outside Environmental Conditions

Refers to environmental health and hygiene factors (e.g., litter, garbage, vermin, clutter, odors around the exterior of the home) that are NOT WITHIN the family's control. Need to consider intervening with owner/landlord, county health department, city code enforcement, and/or other regulatory agencies.

Score	Operational Definition
1	Consistently clean and orderly; property very well maintained by owner/landlord and other tenants if a rental
1.5	
2	Generally clean and orderly; no health hazards; property well maintained by owner/landlord and other tenants if a rental
2.5	
3	Some lack of cleanliness; some disorderliness or clutter; other tenants or neighbors create messiness; slow response to problems by owner/landlord; occasional roach problem
3.5	
4	Inadequately clean or organized; potential health hazards present; a great deal of clutter or litter/garbage; or offensive odors; consistent roach problem; property poorly maintained by owner/landlord and other tenants; very difficult to reach or get response from owner/landlord
4.5	
5	Health hazards and violations present, e.g., overflowing trash bins/barrels, rotting food, flies; multiple vermin present; property essentially ignored by owner/landlord; other tenants do not do their part to maintain clean, healthy environment

STRENGTHS:

CONCERNS:

A2. Cleanliness/Orderliness—Outside Home Maintenance

Refers to environmental health and hygiene factors (e.g., litter, garbage, vermin, clutter, odors around the exterior of the home) that ARE WITHIN the family's ability to control. Assesses family's willingness and ability to maintain clean, orderly environment.

Score	Operational Definition
1	Consistently clean and orderly; family takes very good care of their home or, if an apartment building, takes lead among tenants to keep property clean and neat
1.5	
2	Generally clean and orderly; no health hazards; if in an apartment, family takes good care of area around their unit
2.5	
3	Some lack of cleanliness; some disorderliness or clutter; family does not routinely clean up area around their unit or home
3.5	
4	Inadequately clean or organized; potential health hazards present; a great deal of clutter or litter/garbage, or offensive odors; family rarely cleans-up area around their unit or home
4.5	
5	Health hazards present, e.g., overflowing trash bins/barrels, rotting food, toxins exposed; family does nothing to clean up area around their unit or home, or contributes to lack of cleanliness/orderliness

STRENGTHS:

CONCERNS:

* The term *home* is used to denote any dwelling in which the family may live, including but not limited to a single family home, town home, apartment, and shelter.

A3. Cleanliness/Orderliness—Inside Home Maintenance

Refers to litter, garbage, cleanliness, feces, vermin, clutter, and odors in home. Does not refer to cleanliness of people in home. Assesses health hazards and physical neglect issues that ARE WITHIN the family's control.

STRENGTHS:

1	Consistently clean and orderly; family takes very good care of their home
1.5	
2	Generally clean and orderly; family takes good care of their home
2.5	
3	Some lack of cleanliness and orderliness, e.g., some clutter, trash, full garbage bags, noticeable but tolerable odor; occasional roach problem due to lack of cleaning; could be improved with a couple of hours of work
3.5	

CONCERNS:

4	Generally not clean and orderly, e.g., food particles on floors, tables, chairs; dirty diapers laying around; consistent odors; grease and grime evident; potential health hazard; consistent roach problem despite fumigation
4.5	
5	Extremely dirty, e.g., multiple vermin, urine-soaked furniture, sticky floors, feces on floor, rotting food, overflowing garbage, intolerable odors; health hazards present

A4. Safety—Outside Environmental Conditions

Refers to condition of building in terms of danger as well as functioning of utilities. If a rental, assesses conditions that are generally NOT WITHIN family's control.

STRENGTHS:

1	Building in consistently safe condition; extra safety precautions provided (e.g., locks, good lighting, clear access); property very well maintained by owner/landlord
1.5	
2	Building generally in good condition; some basic safety precautions provided; no obvious problems; property well maintained by owner/landlord
2.5	
3	Some safety concerns present, e.g., cracks in walls, cracked windows, mold on wall, minimal lighting or missing lights, plumbing problems; property minimally maintained by owner/landlord; slow response to problems by owner/landlord
3.5	

CONCERNS:

4	Generally not safe; noticeable safety hazards, e.g., uncovered or unfenced bodies of water, broken windows, rotting floors or walls, poor lighting, blocked access ways, poorly operating elevators, property poorly maintained by owner/landlord; very difficult to reach or get response from owner/landlord
4.5	
5	Extremely dangerous; obvious safety hazards, e.g., broken windows within child(ren)'s reach, holes through walls, missing steps, broken glass in hallways and play area; dangerous materials all around, i.e., rusting metal, broken glass, sharp tools; no exterior lighting; code violations; property essentially ignored by owner/landlord

A5. Safety—Outside Home Maintenance

Refers to caregiver's thoughtfulness as regards to safety precautions. Assesses conditions that ARE WITHIN family's control.

STRENGTHS:

CONCERNS:

Score	Operational Definition
1	Extra safety precautions taken by family, e.g., locks, closed gates, child fencing, guards around rough edges, well organized exterior of home or area around unit
1.5	
2	Good basic safety precautions taken by family no obvious problems; generally organized exterior of home or area around unit
2.5	
3	Some safety concerns present, e.g., unlocked gates, unprotected access to stairwells, balconies; minimal organization of exterior of home or area around unit; minimal precautions taken
3.5	
4	Generally not safe; noticeable safety hazards; poorly organized exterior; dangerous materials accessibility to children, e.g., toxic waste, old freezer, lots of junk; few precautions taken
4.5	
5	Extremely dangerous; obvious safety hazards; no precautions taken

A6. Safety—Inside Home Maintenance

Refers to caregiver's thoughtfulness as regards to safety precautions in the home. Assesses conditions that ARE WITHIN family's control.

STRENGTHS:

CONCERNS:

Score	Operational Definition
1	Extra safety precautions taken, e.g., poisons and medications locked away, outlets plugged; plans for emergency situations; child proofed
1.5	
2	Most precautions taken; no danger to child(ren), e.g., poisons and medications out of reach but not locked; mostly child proofed
2.5	
3	Some precautions taken but potential hazards obvious, e.g., poisons and medications out of sight but within reach of child(ren), overloaded outlets, matches and knives accessible but out of sight; no emergency plans established
3.5	
4	Generally not safe, e.g., poisons and medications visible and accessible, broken glass on floor, wires frayed, no screens on second floor windows for toddlers; few precautions taken
4.5	
5	Extremely dangerous; no apparent safety precautions taken, e.g., many hazards within reach, such as guns, hunting knives, street drugs, open medication bottles

SECTION B: FINANCIAL CONDITIONS

B1. Financial Stress

Refers to degree of financial stress experienced by family regardless of income. Contributing factors might include unemployment, high debts, inadequate income, e.g., AFDC, minimum wage, etc.

STRENGTHS:

CONCERNS:

B2. Financial Management

Refers to ability to plan, budget, organize, and spend money wisely and responsibly.

STRENGTHS:

CONCERNS:

Score	Operational Definition
1	No stress; money not an issue; enough money to meet responsibilities and spend on leisure activities; no employment worries
1.5	
2	Minor stress; manageable debts; some limitations on luxuries but not on necessities
2.5	
3	Consistent worry; just making ends meet, i.e., AFDC, SSI, minimum wage job; income equals debts/bills; working poor
3.5	
4	Very stressful; frequently running out of money; unmanageable debts; unable to stay current on bills/debts; employment worries; suffering emotionally due to financial stress
4.5	
5	Extremely stressful; money problematic on daily basis; necessities not provided; creating significant conflicts in relationships; seems hopeless; "no light at the end of the tunnel"
1	Above average; good at bargain hunting; plans budgets; organizes in a way that gets best value for money and meets family needs consistently
1.5	
2	Minimal and manageable debts; generally has planned use of money; generally spends money wisely
2.5	
3	Some problems in planning or budgeting for use of money; occasional impulse buying; doesn't deprive child of necessities but problem if there is an emergency; limited planning for future needs; debts occasionally unmanageable
3.5	
4	In debt over their heads; irresponsible spending; often buys luxuries rather than necessities; cannot account for money/spending
4.5	
5	No plan or budget for use of money; without necessities; frequently broke; money used for betting, gambling, or alcohol/drugs rather than on family necessities

B3. Financial Problem Due to Welfare System/Child Support

Refers to financial problems that result from errors, delays, etc., in welfare or child support system that are out of client's control.

Score	Operational Definition
1	Not financially dependent on welfare system or child support
1.5	
2	Isolated problems that are quickly resolved or do not create major problems
2.5	
3	Regular problems with eligibility worker or other responsible caregiver
3.5	
4	Irregular or late AFDC, Medi-Cal or food stamps; child support sporadic
4.5	
5	Severe problems; little hope of resolution; causes extreme financial difficulty for family; canceled aid; not eligible; absent caregiver provides no child support

STRENGTHS:

CONCERNS:

B4. Adequate Furniture

Refers to amount of furniture and whether or not it meets the needs of the family; also refers to condition of the furniture.

Score	Operational Definition
1	Above average; new or in excellent condition
1.5	
2	Basic, sufficient furniture for family needs; functional; good condition
2.5	
3	Limited amount of furniture; meets some but not all family needs; fair condition
3.5	
4	Sparse furnishings; furniture generally inadequate in meeting family needs; only able to sleep on floor; missing furniture but may have luxuries; no furniture in some rooms; broken, nonfunctional furniture
4.5	
5	Inadequate furnishings; does not meet family needs, e.g., missing necessities, nothing to sit on, one bed for entire family; furniture presents health or safety hazard

STRENGTHS:

CONCERNS:

B5. Availability of Transportation

Refers to availability or access to a car, bus, or rides.

Score	Operational Definition
1	No problem with transportation
1.5	
2	Adequate access to transportation
2.5	
3	Limited access to reliable transportation
3.5	
4	Minimal access to reliable transportation
4.5	
5	Transportation unavailable and presents a major problem

STRENGTHS:

CONCERNS:

SECTION C: SUPPORTS TO CAREGIVERS

C1. Support from Friends and Neighbors and Community Involvement

Refers to involvements/connections in society and community that offer positive support for family.

Score	Operational Definition
STRENGTHS:	
1	Maintains strong support and reciprocal network of friends and neighbors; active in community; regularly attends community functions (e.g., church, recreational, cultural)
1.5	
2	Adequate social support; friends or neighbors supportive; some community involvement
2.5	
3	Limited social support; few friends or only acquaintances; seeks or offers no concrete help from people; goes to community resources in crisis; occasional contact in community (e.g., school, church)
3.5	
CONCERNS:	
4	Minimal social support; limited friendships; no connection with neighbors or neighbors nonexistent; very limited social/community contact
4.5	
5	No friends; extremely isolated; negative impact or involvement; leaves home for necessities only; may not leave home at all

C2. Available Child Care

Refers to availability, affordability, and adequacy of child care. Note: If caregiver says, "I never leave my child" question why: Past problems? Current resources?

Score	Operational Definition
STRENGTHS:	
1	Available and affordable; relative, other person, or child care provider willingly provides good care
1.5	
2	Some difficulty finding and affording good child care, but has adequate resources
2.5	
3	Caregiver not always available or affordable as needed; baby sitter/ relative/friend does it but complains
3.5	
CONCERNS:	
4	Rarely able to find available, affordable, adequate child care
4.5	
5	None; no family, friends, neighbors; no child care; no money for it

C3. Chooses Appropriate Substitute Caregivers

Refers to caregiver's planning for safe and appropriate child care. Keep in mind age appropriateness and need of child(ren). If no money, resources, or adequate child care available, indicate N/A and make note in comments as to what problem is, so it can be addressed.

STRENGTHS:

CONCERNS:

Score	Operational Definition
1	Caregiver very careful and conscientious; checks things out, e.g., obtains and talks with references; makes sure child(ren) is comfortable and safe with substitute caregiver
1.5	
2	Generally adequate and careful about child care decisions; concerns may exist but do not create risk
2.5	
3	Inconsistencies in decisions about child care (e.g., sometimes for convenience v. appropriateness); some pattern of questionable decisions, e.g., leaves young child(ren) with inappropriate caregivers; leaves child(ren) at home alone for periods essentially unsupervised
3.5	
4	Leaves child(ren) in chaotic care situations; physical care all right but emotional deprivation or cruelty suffered; left with casual acquaintances; relies on known drug or alcohol users as caregivers
4.5	
5	No thinking about or planning for child care; child(ren) left with strangers or known child abuser; child(ren) left totally alone with no supervision or anyone watching over; child(ren) left with person currently under the influence of drugs or alcohol

C4. Available Health Care

Refers to availability, affordability, and accessibility of health care.

STRENGTHS:

CONCERNS:

Score	Operational Definition
1	Comprehensive health care (including dental care) available, affordable, and accessible, e.g., private insurance, HMO, Medi-Cal with medical home
1.5	
2	Adequate availability and access to affordable health care including preventive care, e.g., immunizations, well-child care, dental care
2.5	
3	Limited availability and access to affordable health care; only go to doctor when sick; difficulty affording prescription medication; generally uses same medical care providers, e.g., local community clinic
3.5	
4	Minimal availability and access to affordable health care; no form of insurance making cost very prohibitive; uses emergency rooms for routine care; has to wait too long to seek medical care due to lack of money
4.5	
5	No access, availability, or ability to afford health care of any kind

C5. Provides for Basic Medical/Physical Care

Refers to caregiver's provision of good home health care; good nutrition; personal hygiene; as well as caregiver's accessing and follow-through on preventive well-child medical care and treatment. This item refers to issues that ARE WITHIN the ability of the caregiver to control, influence or change.

STRENGTHS:

Score	Definition
1	Very attentive to health care and hygiene issues; nutritionally planned meals; child(ren) receive routine well-child medical care and immunizations are current; child(ren) receive routine preventive dental care
1.5	
2	Adequate medical and physical care provided; caregiver generally reacts appropriately to symptoms of illness; generally keeps regularly scheduled checkups/appointments; adequate nutrition, grooming, and hygiene
2.5	

CONCERNS:

Score	Definition
3	Occasional problems; inadequate home health care practices; child(ren) often sick; immunization not on schedule; limited attention to nutrition; inconsistent personal hygiene or appropriate dress for the weather; do not receive preventive dental care
3.5	
4	Minimal attention to medical/physical care; generally inadequate; poor home health care practices or practices have potential for harm; waits too long to go to doctor when child(ren) is sick; child(ren) has not been immunized; poor follow-through on recommended treatment
4.5	
5	Child(ren)'s health is endangered; extremely inadequate home health care, e.g., food, clothing, malnutrition, inappropriate clothing for weather; child(ren) not receiving needed medical care; appearance of failure to thrive

C6. Ability to Maintain Long-Term Relationship

Refers to quality, length, and emotional support of adult-to-adult relationships including friends and partners (not of family origin).

Caregiver* Score A	B	Operational Definition

STRENGTHS:

A	B	Operational Definition
1	1	Lots of friends; no problem maintaining emotionally supportive intimate relationship with occasional normal conflict
1.5	1.5	
2	2	Has experienced long-term friendship or intimate relationship; several good friends
2.5	2.5	

CONCERNS:

A	B	Operational Definition
3	3	A long-term conflictive relationship or multiple short-term partners; minimal social relationships
3.5	3.5	
4	4	History of sporadic relationships or long-term conflictive relationship with no network of friends
4.5	4.5	
5	5	No past or current intimate relationships; no personal friendships

* Rate each caregiver separately unless otherwise specified.

SECTION D: CAREGIVER/CHILD INTERACTIONS

D1. Understands Child Development

Refers to all areas of development including physical, emotional, cognitive, and social.

	Caregiver Score		Operational Definition
	A	B	
STRENGTHS:	1	1	Above average understanding of child(ren) and child development
	1.5	1.5	
	2	2	Adequate knowledge of child development leading to age appropriate expectations
	2.5	2.5	
	3	3	Limited knowledge in some areas leading to parental frustration over age-typical child behavior
	3.5	3.5	
CONCERNS:	4	4	Limited understanding; could place child(ren) at high risk for emotional and/or physical abuse or neglect; sees problems that are not there; has unrealistic expectations of child(ren)
	4.5	4.5	
	5	5	Little knowledge or inappropriate understanding of child development which has resulted in some type of abuse or neglect

D2. Daily Routine for Child(ren)

Refers to all areas of child(ren)'s life such as bedtime, meals, naps, homework, baths, etc.

	Caregiver Score		Operational Definition
	A	B	
STRENGTHS:	1	1	Consistent routine for child(ren) that is age appropriate and recognizes individual differences
	1.5	1.5	
	2	2	Reasonably consistent, flexible, and age appropriate daily routines
	2.5	2.5	
	3	3	Has some daily routines; some inconsistency or rigidity
	3.5	3.5	
CONCERNS:	4	4	Minimal routine with little consistency or overly rigid or overly permissive
	4.5	4.5	
	5	5	No routine; no consistency; no flexibility

D3. Use of Physical Discipline

Refers to use, frequency, and severity of physical punishment. Assess for age and vulnerability of child(ren) and potential for harm.

Rating	Description
STRENGTHS:	
1 – 1.5	Only uses nonphysical forms of discipline
2 – 2.5	Generally does not use physical discipline but may infrequently swat with hand or spank
3 – 3.5	Uses physical discipline in response to specific behaviors; spanking, pinching, pulling ears or hair
CONCERNS:	
4 – 4.5	Regular use of physical punishment which could endanger child(ren)'s safety; use of belts, shoes; throws things at child
5	Regular and severe physical punishment; explosive and out of control; shaking of infants or toddlers; behavior endangers child(ren)'s safety

D4. Appropriateness of Disciplinary Methods

Refers to a planned approach appropriate to child(ren)'s age; caregiver is in emotional control and uses discipline to teach rather than punish.

Rating	Description
STRENGTHS:	
1 – 1.5	Well thought out, age appropriate, nonpunitive educational approach; uses variety of positive techniques as part of regular routine
2 – 2.5	Generally practices rules, natural consequences, positive reinforcement when disciplining; caregiver in emotional control
3 – 3.5	Some inappropriate expectations; some potential for emotional or physical harm, tendency to focus on negative aspects of child(ren)'s behavior, i.e., "serves you right" attitude; sometimes ignores child(ren) inappropriately; sometimes does not discipline when needed
CONCERNS:	
4 – 4.5	Unplanned punitive approach; mostly reacts emotionally and with inappropriate age expectations; emotionally abusive; overreacts to behaviors and situations; rarely sees positive in child(ren); does not discipline most of the time; means of discipline has great potential for harm
5	Past or current severe emotional and/or physical abuse or no discipline at all

D5. Consistency of Discipline

Refers to predictability; child(ren) has been made aware of consequences and feels secure about caregiver's response. Misbehavior is corrected each time it occurs and in a similar manner.

	Caregiver Score		Operational Definition
	A	B	
STRENGTHS:	1	1	Well thought out consistent plan appropriate for situation; not negatively impacted by caregiver's mood or stress level
	1.5	1.5	
	2	2	Generally consistent and predictable response to behavior; appropriate to age and situation; infrequently impacted by caregiver's mood
	2.5	2.5	
CONCERNS:	3	3	Some consistency; caregivers unaware of importance of consistency; occasionally dependent on caregiver's mood; sometimes inappropriate for age or situation
	3.5	3.5	
	4	4	Mostly inconsistent or unpredictable; little flexibility related to age or situation; mostly dependent on caregiver's mood or stress level
	4.5	4.5	
	5	5	No consistency or predictability; no flexibility related to age or situation; totally dependent on caregiver's mood or stress level

D6. Bonding Style with Child(ren)

Refers to emotional investment and attachment of the caregiver to the child(ren).

	Caregiver Score		Operational Definition
	A	B	
STRENGTHS:	1	1	Encourages appropriate attachment and independence; attentive; responds appropriately to needs; reads child(ren)'s cues correctly; sends consistent messages to child(ren)
	1.5	1.5	
	2	2	Adequate emotional involvement and support; occasional difficulty allowing separation/differences; reads cues correctly most of the time
	2.5	2.5	
CONCERNS:	3	3	Some inconsistency in emotional support; some ambivalence; responds to physical and/or social needs inconsistency; difficulty reading child(ren)'s cues; some over involvement or lack of appropriate involvement
	3.5	3.5	
	4	4	Minimal responsiveness to child(ren)'s needs; little emotional investment; irritable; over-identifying; often misinterprets cues; frequently does not respond or responds inappropriately; minimal response to child(ren)'s approach/attachment to other people
	4.5	4.5	
	5	5	Inappropriate attachment (e.g., unable to see child(ren) as separate individual); resentful; rejecting; detached; promotes child(ren)'s attachment to other people rather than self; child(ren) endangered by nonresponsive or inappropriate responses; total lack of involvement with child(ren)

D7. Attitude Expressed About Child(ren)/Caregiver Role

Refers to verbal or nonverbal behaviors indicating enjoyment of the child(ren) and parenting. Assesses degree to which caregiver accepts child(ren) as he/she is without projecting either positive or negative attitudes about or onto the child(ren).

STRENGTHS:

CONCERNS:

		Description
1	1	Happy to have parental role; sees humor in parenting; accepting; warm; loving; positive; has realistic view of challenges and rewards
1.5	1.5	
2	2	Generally positive; accepts parental role; verbalizes some enjoyment most of the time
2.5	2.5	
3	3	Inconsistent view of parenting; mostly views child(ren) as responsibility; limited moments of enjoyment in parenting; some indifference; some irritation and resentment; attitude depends on mood
3.5	3.5	
4	4	Primarily negative view of parenting; feelings of being tied down; no pleasure; ambivalent; predominantly irritated and resentful; minimal expression of love or acceptance of child(ren)
4.5	4.5	
5	5	Negative view of parental role; child(ren) seen as obstacle in caregiver's life; resents responsibility or parenting and parenting tasks; detached and indifferent or rejecting; no desire to fulfill parenting role

D8. Takes Appropriate Authority Role

Refers to caregiver's ability to convey and accept appropriate authority.

STRENGTHS:

CONCERNS:

		Description
1	1	Consistently demonstrates ability to exercise appropriate authority; willing and able to negotiate on privileges and consequences appropriate to child(ren)'s age and situation; caregiver knows how and when to set and hold limits
1.5	1.5	
2	2	Generally consistent in exercise of appropriate authority; occasional power struggle; can usually set and hold limits
2.5	2.5	
3	3	Some inconsistency in setting limits and structure; arbitrarily exercises authority
3.5	3.5	
4	4	Seldom exercises appropriate authority; minimal limit setting; seldom maintains limits set; frequent role reversal; constant power struggles; caregiver unable to say no or allow child(ren) any decision-making power; child(ren) mostly sets own rules
4.5	4.5	Demonstrates no ability to exercise appropriate authority; no structure or limits; complete role reversal; abdicates responsibility
5	5	

D9. Quality and Effectiveness of Communication [Caregiver to Child(ren)]

Refers to caregiver's ability not only to make own desires known but foster child(ren)'s understanding and communication abilities.

Caregiver Score A	Caregiver Score B	Operational Definition
STRENGTHS:		
1	1	Open two-way verbal communication without fear; praises and supports appropriately
1.5	1.5	
2	2	Generally good communication with some difficulty verbalizing in some areas (i.e., sex, deep feelings); usually supportive; sometimes does not listen to child(ren)'s attempt to communicate; no verbal abuse
2.5	2.5	
CONCERNS:		
3	3	Limited communication; gives some mixed messages; some ignoring or discounting of child(ren)'s attempt to communicate; some criticism of child(ren)
3.5	3.5	
4	4	Minimal communication; primarily negative, harsh, and ineffective; or child(ren) is discouraged from communicating thoughts or feelings; rarely supportive
4.5	4.5	
5	5	Communication is negative, critical, and abusive; child(ren) not allowed to talk about feelings; or absence of verbal communication; nonsupportive

D10. Quality and Effectiveness of Communication [Child(ren) to Caregiver]

Refers to child(ren)'s verbal or nonverbal ability to communicate needs and feelings to caregiver.

Caregiver Score A	Caregiver Score B	Operational Definition
STRENGTHS:		
1	1	Open verbal communication and appropriate affection; child(ren) able to express feelings and needs
1.5	1.5	
2	2	Child(ren) can generally communicate feelings and needs appropriately
2.5	2.5	
3	3	Child(ren) has some difficulty communicating own feelings and needs to caregiver(s); hesitant in initiation and response; gives only brief answers; sometimes ignores caregivers
3.5	3.5	
CONCERNS:		
4	4	Extremely limited ability to communicate; frequently ignores or verbally provokes caregivers; frightened or withdrawn; rarely shares ideas, feelings, or needs with caregiver
4.5	4.5	
5	5	No effective or constructive communication with caregiver; constant fighting or provoking or active avoidance or verbally abusive towards caregiver

D11. Cooperation/Follows Rules and Directions

Refers to degree to which child(ren) follows rules and directions and is a cooperative member of the family.

STRENGTHS:

		Description
1	1	Consistently cooperative; follows rules and directions established by caregivers
1.5	1.5	
2	2	Mostly cooperative; generally follows rules and directions established by caregivers
2.5	2.5	
3	3	Inconsistently cooperative; needs frequent reminding to follow rules and directions
3.5	3.5	

CONCERNS:

		Description
4	4	Mostly uncooperative; seldom abides by rules and directions established by caregivers
4.5	4.5	
5	5	Uncooperative; refuses to follow rules or directions established by caregivers

D12. Bonding to Caregiver

Refers to child(ren)'s emotional attachment to caregiver(s). To help in assessing, note to whom the child(ren) seems most bonded and the qualities of the attachment. These qualities can be seen in language, facial expressions, tone of voice, content of communications, visual contact, physical closeness or distance and amount of time spent with the caregiver and depends on the developmental stage of the child(ren)).

STRENGTHS:

		Description
1	1	Child(ren) exhibit consistently appropriate attachment and bonding to caregiver
1.5	1.5	
2	2	Child(ren) exhibit adequate bonding; show occasional tensions or anxieties
2.5	2.5	
3	3	Child(ren) exhibit some signs of ambivalence, anxiety or hostility toward caregiver; child(ren) may demonstrate insecure attachment (e.g., may appear overly needy)
3.5	3.5	

CONCERNS:

		Description
4	4	Minimal appropriate attachment with caregiver; behavior indicates anger, uncertainty, reluctance, or indifference toward caregiver; child(ren) may seem needy of attention from strangers
4.5	4.5	
5	5	Inappropriate attachment; child(ren) exhibit extreme dependence or independence; consistently hostile, rejecting or provocative stance towards caregiver; or excessive fearfulness of caregiver; or indiscriminate attachment to strangers

SECTION E: DEVELOPMENTAL STIMULATION

E1. Appropriate Play Area/Things—Inside Home

Refers to adequacy and safety of play area; number and condition of playthings; age appropriateness or developmental appropriateness of playthings.

Score	Operational Definition
STRENGTHS:	
1	Child safe play area present; a wide choice of age appropriate learning playthings in good and safe condition available
1.5	
2	Age appropriate learning playthings generally available; adequate play area generally available
2.5	
3	Some age appropriate learning playthings for each child; limited play area with some potential dangers
3.5	
CONCERNS:	
4	Very limited or no playthings available; play items in poor condition or unsafe; very limited or unsafe play area available
4.5	
5	Nothing to play with; or inappropriate/potentially dangerous items used as playthings; no play area available

E2. Provides Enriching/Learning Experiences for Child(ren)

Refers to caregiver's investment in child(ren) social and academic growth and development.

Caregiver Score A	B	Operational Definition
STRENGTHS:		
1	1	Interacts with enjoyment; plans reading or story telling time; carefully selects experiences; plans outings (i.e., park, museum); avid involvement with school; appropriately help to attain expected developmental tasks (i.e., walking, talking, self-care skills)
1.5	1.5	
2	2	Reads to child(ren) as time allows; monitors what child(ren) watches on TV; occasionally planned learning activity; checks homework; talks to teacher
2.5	2.5	
3	3	Inconsistently provides enriching learning experiences; lets kids watch any program on TV, although may verbally disapprove; interacts with school only at school's request; rarely reads to child(ren); allows child(ren) to develop with minimal guidance and/or with unrealistic expectations (i.e., child must read before starting school)
3.5	3.5	
CONCERNS:		
4	4	Little interest in child(ren)'s activities, learning, and development; avoids school contact; child(ren) on own or excessive pressure to achieve
4.5	4.5	
5	5	Blocks and rejects child(ren)'s need for learning; keeps child(ren) at home to meet own needs; interferes with child(ren)'s attempts to achieve normal developmental tasks (i.e., keeps child in crib 90% of the time, holds excessively, only talks baby talk); or pressures child(ren) to perform/achieve to degree that child(ren) develops emotional or physical problems

E3. Ability and Time for Child(ren)'s Play

Refers to caregiver's understanding of the value of play and creating or allowing it.

STRENGTHS:

1	1.5	Understands importance of play; sets aside time; plays with child(ren); encourages playfulness and spontaneity; encourages creative play
1.5	2	
2	2.5	Understands the value of children's play; sometimes sets up play situation; or sometimes makes helpful suggestions regarding play activities; or plays with children occasionally as time allows
2.5	3	

CONCERNS:

3	3.5	Sees little importance in play; seldom plays with child(ren) but allows child(ren) to play; some dampening of spontaneity
3.5	4	Ignores child(ren)'s need for play; makes no provisions for space or time; doesn't play with child(ren); puts unnecessary restrictions on play; puts down spontaneity; feels children should be working or studying rather than playing
4	4.5	
4.5	5	Resents need for play; thwarts playfulness and spontaneity in child; "I never got to play, all he/she ever does is play"; does not want or allow child(ren) to play
5		

E4. Deals with Sibling Interactions

Refers to caregiver's ability to cope with sibling conflicts and structure positive interaction. Mark N/A if no siblings.

STRENGTHS:

1	1.5	Aware and sensitive to sibling interactions; teaches problem solving appropriate sharing and respect; appreciates individual differences; fairness is important
1.5	2	
2	2.5	Limits fighting; encourages appropriate sharing and verbal conflict resolution; generally assists with problem solving; tries to be fair
2.5	3	

CONCERNS:

3	3.5	Inconsistent; sometimes assists with conflicts and problem solving; fairness not generally considered important
3.5	4	Indifferent; leaves to own devices; tends to ignore sibling interaction both positive and negative; or does not treat children equitably
4	4.5	
4.5	5	Favors or rejects one; or fosters rivalry; or scapegoats one child; or allows one to rule; or compares children negatively
5		

SECTION F: INTERACTIONS BETWEEN CAREGIVERS

F1. Conjoint Problem Solving Ability

Refers to the ability of caregivers to listen, develop options, and compromise (rate ability of all caregivers in household, not each caregiver).

STRENGTHS:

CONCERNS:

Score	Operational Definition
1	Consistently able to negotiate and communicate; encourage each other to give and express own opinion
1.5	
2	Generally able to negotiate; occasional difficulty in developing options or listening to each other
2.5	
3	Limited communication skills; able to problem solve some daily living issues (i.e., shopping, home chores), but difficulty solving bigger issues (i.e., children, relatives)
3.5	
4	Rarely able to problem solve together; decision-making discussions become arguments
4.5	
5	No compromise or negotiation; problems are not discussed

F2. Manner of Dealing with Conflicts/Stress

Refers to way in which caregivers handle conflicts (rate ability of all caregivers in household, not each caregiver).

STRENGTHS:

CONCERNS:

Score	Operational Definition
1	Constructively talk over problems; effective handling of stress/conflict
1.5	
2	Discuss major differences; most conflicts resolved; occasionally arguing
2.5	
3	Major conflicts ignored and remain unresolved; able to resolve minor differences; frequent arguing; some verbal threats and intimidation used
3.5	
4	Constant disagreement; arguing; occasionally resort to physical expression like slamming doors, breaking things but not physically abusive towards each other
4.5	
5	Incapable of dealing with conflict effectively; resorts to negative behaviors, e.g., domestic violence, substance abuse, abandonment, harmful to emotional and physical health and safety of self and others

F3. Balance of Power

Refers to healthy interdependence (rate caregivers together, not each caregiver).

	Score	Operational Definition
STRENGTHS:	1	Distribution of power is functional within context of family
	1.5	
	2	Minor imbalance; "traditional roles" accepted by both caregivers (i.e., culturally accepted roles)
	2.5	
CONCERNS:	3	Some imbalance leading to some difficulty in problem solving and conflict resolution; some emotional distress exhibited due to nature of interdependent roles
	3.5	
	4	Major imbalance; high risk for domestic violence; emotionally harmful; one extremely domineering
	4.5	
	5	Severe imbalance; detrimental to physical and emotional well-being of children or adults; one extremely victimized or dominated; presence of domestic violence

F4. Supportive

Refers to emotional support and degree to which caregivers can count on each other (rate each caregiver separately).

	Caregiver Score		Operational Definition
	A	B	
STRENGTHS:	1	1	Supportive; responsible; appreciative; encouraging
	1.5	1.5	
	2	2	Mostly supportive and encouraging; minor disagreements or disappointments where partner might feel criticized
	2.5	2.5	
CONCERNS:	3	3	Limited and inconsistent support; unpredictable; unknowingly hurtful
	3.5	3.5	
	4	4	Minimal support; frequently unreliable; irresponsible; often lets partner down; frequently does not backup partner; critical
	4.5	4.5	
	5	5	Does no follow through on agreements; unreliable; extremely critical of other; insults partner in public; ridicules partner

F5. Caregivers' Attitude Toward Each Other

Refers to overall feelings partners seem to have about each other (rate each caregiver separately).

Caregiver Score A	Caregiver Score B	Operational Definition
STRENGTHS:		
1.5	1	Respectful; positive; admiring; caring; appreciative of differences; trusting
	1.5	
2	2	Generally supportive and encouraging; warm; occasionally feels some minor irritation with partner
2.5	2.5	
CONCERNS:		
3	3	Some indifference; irritation; patronizing; ambivalence
3.5	3.5	
4	4	Condescending; resentful; angry; disrespectful; fearful
4.5	4.5	
5	5	Excessively fearful; abusive; hostile; hateful; rejecting; totally indifferent

F6. Ability to Communicate (Verbal and Nonverbal)

Refers to ability and/or willingness to listen to the other and express oneself (rate each caregiver separately).

Caregiver Score A	Caregiver Score B	Operational Definition
STRENGTHS:		
1	1	Open communication; able to express opinions or feelings, or experiences comfortably and safely
1.5	1.5	
2	2	Generally adequate; minor difficulties communicating on certain issues; willing to communicate actively
2.5	2.5	
CONCERNS:		
3	3	Limited communication; daily life/business oriented; minimal personal conversation; minimal hearing of feelings; nonproductive communication of important issues; tendency to withdraw
3.5	3.5	
4	4	Minimal communication; very poor communication; a lot of misunderstanding; misreading of other's cues; mostly unwilling to listen to other's opinions
4.5	4.5	
5	5	No communication; no ability or willingness to listen or express opinions or feelings

Caregiver History and Characteristics

Sections G through H

SECTION G: CAREGIVER HISTORY

G1. Stability/Adequacy of Caregiver's Childhood

Refers to stability, consistency/continuity, and emotional adequacy of caregiver's own upbringing during childhood.

	Caregiver Score		Operational Definition
	A	B	
STRENGTHS:	1	1	Self-worth and individualization were supported and fostered by own parents; received consistent and stable caregiving
	1.5	1.5	
	2	2	Some instability during childhood, but not enough to cause problems; received adequate emotional support and nurturing
	2.5	2.5	
CONCERNS:	3	3	Received limited nurturing; traumatic loss of contact with one parent; physically or emotionally remote parent(s); somewhat conflictual relationship with parent(s) as a child
	3.5	3.5	
	4	4	Little or no nurturing; changing parental figures; long-term parental absence; chronically tumultuous relationship with parent(s) as child
	4.5	4.5	
	5	5	Mainly raised in foster home(s) or institution(s)

G2. Childhood History of Physical Abuse/Corporal Punishment

Refers to use of corporal punishment, severity, and physical abuse by caregiver's parents during childhood.

	Caregiver Score		Operational Definition
	A	B	
STRENGTHS:	1	1	None
	1.5	1.5	
	2	2	Occasional spanking, not the routine method of punishment
	2.5	2.5	
CONCERNS:	3	3	Spanking was regular method of discipline; occasional incidents of excessive corporal punishment
	3.5	3.5	
	4	4	Routine excessive corporal punishment; physical abuse; hit with fist or objects
	4.5	4.5	
	5	5	Life-threatening physical abuse; hospitalization

G3. Childhood History of Sexual Abuse

Refers to degree of sexual abuse experienced.

Caregiver Score A	Caregiver Score B	Operational Definition
		STRENGTHS:
1	1	Parents proactively taught self-protection skills
1.5	1.5	
2	2	No exposure to inappropriate sexuality
2.5	2.5	
3	3	Some inappropriate exposure to sexuality
		CONCERNS:
3.5	3.5	
4	4	Incidents of exposure to sexual activity (fondling, flashing, oral sex) causing confusion and/or problem, but no physical force or threat involved
4.5	4.5	
5	5	One or more traumatic events, e.g., rape, incest, sodomy, oral copulation, chronic long-term sexual abuse; physical force or threat involved

G4. History of Substance Abuse

Refers to use and abuse of alcohol and/or drugs in the past.

Caregiver Score A	Caregiver Score B	Operational Definition
		STRENGTHS:
1	1	None; never used anything
1.5	1.5	
2	2	Social, recreational use or experimentation; no resulting social/emotional problems
2.5	2.5	
3	3	Frequent pattern of abuse resulting in social/emotional problems; currently recovering in or out of a program
		CONCERNS:
3.5	3.5	
4	4	Routine use, e.g., every weekend or daily use
4.5	4.5	
5	5	Chronic addiction; daily use over time

G5. History of Aggressive Act as an Adult

Refers to severity of physically violent acts toward people or property. Assesses propensity toward violence.

STRENGTHS / CONCERNS	Score	Description
STRENGTHS:	1 / 1.5	History of appropriate assertiveness; no history of verbal assaults
	2 / 2.5	No aggressive/violent acts
	3 / 3.5	Tantrum-like behavior which may have resulted in minimal property damage, but not directed at people (e.g., throwing objects; verbal threatening); no child abuse
CONCERNS:	4 / 4.5	History of property damage; fighting with peers; physically threatening; pushing, shoving, shaking people
	5	Beating of people, causing injury or serious property damage

G6. History of Being an Adult Victim

Refers to being victimized as an adult either emotionally or physically.

STRENGTHS / CONCERNS	Score	Description
STRENGTHS:	1 / 1.5	Never a victim
	2 / 2.5	Isolated incident, e.g., mugged, robbed by a stranger
	3 / 3.5	Moderate verbal abuse as in hurtful teasing or name calling; constant put downs by spouse or family member; some pushing or shoving in relationships
CONCERNS:	4 / 4.5	Chronic verbal or emotional abuse; isolated serious incidents of physical abuse, e.g., violent rape or domestic violence; regularly physically threatened, pushed and/or shoved in relationships; pattern of serious incidents of domestic violence resulting in injury
	5	Chronic, consistent victim; puts self in life-threatening situations and/or exploitative relationships; allows self to be used as a prostitute, drug runner, etc.; domestic violence resulting in hospitalization; multiple rapes

G7. Occupational History

Refers to history of occupation/work for pay. Write N/A if a homemaker.

		Description
STRENGTHS:	1 — 1.5	Has career; history of promotions and upward movement in field
	2 — 2.5	Long-term full-time employment
	3 — 3.5	Long-term part-time employment; some pattern or consistency in types of jobs; intermittent employment; frequent unemployed periods
CONCERNS:	4 — 4.5	Irregular jobs; seasonal jobs; disabled; unable to hold job for more than six months; work doing anything to survive
	5 — 5	Chronic unemployment

G8. Extended Family Support

Refers to emotional, social, and concrete help provided by family. Also assesses positive or negative nature of the relationship(s).

		Description
STRENGTHS:	1 — 1.5	Family is positive influence and lives nearby
	2 — 2.5	Family is positive influence but lives far away
	3 — 3.5	Minimal support; a few or one relative(s) nearby; emotional support but no concrete help
CONCERNS:	4 — 4.5	No extended family or no follow-through on commitments
	5 — 5	Negative influence or effect by extended family involvement; more trouble than help

SECTION H: CAREGIVER PERSONAL CHARACTERISTICS

H1. Learning Ability/Style

Refers to ability to understand instructions, directions, ideas, etc. Assesses motivation to learn.

	Caregiver Score		Operational Definition
STRENGTHS:	A	B	
	1	1	Above average; quickly catches on to complex and/or abstract ideas; has ability to anticipate consequences; able to learn through any means
	1.5	1.5	
	2	2	Average; generally understands; minimal repetition/explanation needed for complex and/or abstract idea; able to learn from a variety of means
	2.5	2.5	
CONCERNS:	3	3	A little slow to comprehend; concrete thinking; understands simple concepts, but has problems understanding abstract ideas
	3.5	3.5	
	4	4	Mildly to moderately retarded; difficulty in understanding simple concepts; moderate to major learning disabilities
	4.5	4.5	
	5	5	Thought disorder; severely retarded; minimal comprehension; severe learning disability

H2. Paranoia/Ability to Trust

Refers to degree of paranoia or ability to trust.

	Caregiver Score		Operational Definition
STRENGTHS:	A	B	
	1	1	No paranoia; generally tends to trust within appropriate and realistic limits
	1.5	1.5	
	2	2	A little cautious or overly trusting on occasion
	2.5	2.5	
	3	3	Guarded; has difficulty trusting; question staff's need to know certain basic things; or tends to trust and divulge too quickly
CONCERNS:	3.5	3.5	
	4	4	Suspicious; extreme difficulty trusting; hesitant to reveal any information; or over trusting of strangers; suspiciousness or over trustfulness that causes major problem(s) for person or family
	4.5	4.5	
	5	5	Extreme paranoia; client feels everyone is against him/her without basis in reality; or inappropriate and dangerous trusting of strangers (that threatens own or child(ren)'s welfare)

CAREGIVER HISTORY AND CHARACTERISTICS

H3. Current Substance Use

Refers to current use and abuse of alcohol and/or other drugs.

	Caregiver Score		Operational Definition
	A	B	
STRENGTHS:	1	1	No use
	1.5	1.5	Social, recreational use or experimentation; no interference with daily functioning
	2	2	
	2.5	2.5	Frequent use or experimentation; some current interference in functioning; recovering (in or out of a program)
	3	3	
CONCERNS:	3.5	3.5	
	4	4	Daily, habitual use and abuse; significant interference in ability to function
	4.5	4.5	
	5	5	Chronic addiction; unable to function without drugs or alcohol

H4. Passivity/Helplessness/Dependence

Refers to emotional dependence on someone as well as ability to make daily decisions, write checks, buy food, fulfill job expectations, etc.

	Caregiver Score		Operational Definition
	A	B	
STRENGTHS:	1	1	Functions independently for daily living needs; appropriate emotional independence
	1.5	1.5	
	2	2	Minor areas of dependence
	2.5	2.5	
	3	3	Relies on others for routine help; some emotional dependence; does not like being alone; prefers to be in company of others and vigorously seeks a companion; uses child(ren) for companionship
CONCERNS:	3.5	3.5	
	4	4	Minimal independent functioning; cannot live alone; needs help with money management, buying food; uses child(ren) for emotional support; is easily exploited
	4.5	4.5	
	5	5	Unable to function independently; cannot survive without outside help; requires help with all daily activities; totally emotionally dependent on other(s); stays in relationships at whatever cost to self or child(ren); no independent decision making; pattern of exploitative threatening relationship(s) or living situation(s)

H5. Impulse Control

Refers to ability to tolerate frustration or control destructive acts.

STRENGTHS:

Scale	Description
1 – 1.5	Ability to delay gratification of needs; high level of frustration tolerance
2 – 2.5	Sometimes a little "short-fused" when tired, but does not act out frustration

CONCERNS:

Scale	Description
3 – 3.5	Generally "short-fused" or "high-strung", inconsistent impulse control, e.g., binge eating, drinking, or shopping; slaps child(ren) with hand; yells and screams a lot
4 – 4.5	Very "short-fused"; verbal rages; throws things; often out of control
5	Inadequate impulse control; fights; steals; substance abuse; suicide attempts; hurts self and others; limited ability to care for child(ren)

H6. Cooperation

Refers to degree of cooperation with program measured by actions and statements.

STRENGTHS:

Scale	Description
1 – 1.5	Actively seeking help; provides information with minimal questioning; brings examples of problems; open to new ideas about solutions
2 – 2.5	Willingly cooperates in answering questions; gives additional information; keeps appointments; is punctual; calls to reschedule if necessary; tries suggested ideas

CONCERNS:

Scale	Description
3 – 3.5	Some reluctance or hesitance; needs to be pushed or prodded to give information; passively cooperates; doesn't call if late or to cancel
4 – 4.5	Participates only to please other (or follow court order); comes late; answers questions only "yes" or "no"; give excuses; minimizes problems; refuses to answer some questions
5	No cooperation; refuses to answer most questions; attitude leads to questionable honesty of responses

H7. Emotional Stability (Mood Swings)

Refers to consistency and range of moods or emotions, appropriateness of emotions and/or behavior, speed of reaction. Assesses whether emotions or emotional behavior interfere with daily functioning.

STRENGTHS:

Score		Description
1	1	Emotionally stable
1.5	1.5	
2	2	Occasionally moody with minimal consequences; unaware of feelings; some restricted range
2.5	2.5	
3	3	Moderately moody; significantly limited in emotional range; some inappropriateness in emotional responses; short-tempered; confused circular thinking; mild manic features
3.5	3.5	

CONCERNS:

Score		Description
4	4	Extreme moodiness; unpredictable; frequent inappropriateness that often interferes with functioning
4.5	4.5	
5	5	Grossly inappropriate emotional reaction to situation; emotion interferes consistently with daily life; lack of emotional stability

H8. Depression

Refers to degree of depression and its interference with functioning. Assesses emotional affect, appearance of self and home, level of activity, and verbal statements regarding feelings.

STRENGTHS:

Score		Description
1	1	Not depressed/upbeat attitude toward life
1.5	1.5	
2	2	Periods of mild depression; "feeling blue", but functioning adequately; no impact on child(ren)
2.5	2.5	
3	3	Frequently depressed but functioning without treatment; past suicidal thoughts; "tired" all the time
3.5	3.5	

CONCERNS:

Score		Description
4	4	Seriously depressed but functioning minimally; recent suicidal thoughts; past suicidal attempts or activities intended to hurt self
4.5	4.5	
5	5	Chronic, long-term depression; treated psychiatrically; current suicide attempts; using medication; unable to function currently

H9. Aggression/Anger

Refers to current expressions of aggression and anger.

STRENGTHS:

CONCERNS:

Caregiver Score A	B	Operational Definition
1	1	Above average ability to be assertive; exercises healthy ways of releasing aggressive feelings or anger
1.5	1.5	Adequate; generally appropriate expressions of aggression (i.e., sports, gardening, hobbies, exercise) and anger (i.e., controlled verbal expression not causing physical or emotional harm); occasional verbal barb or slammed door
2	2	
2.5	2.5	Passive aggressive or withholding behaviors; yelling a lot at child(ren); using foul language to excess around child(ren); minimal property damage (i.e., kicking a door)
3	3	
3.5	3.5	Verbally explosive; ranting and raving at child(ren); pattern of provocative statements or behaviors; no injury-causing physical abuse, but harsh (i.e., pushing, pulling, grabbing); more serious property damage (e.g., punching holes in walls); denies anger
4	4	
4.5	4.5	Violent; threatening with some injury-causing physical aggression; threatening abandonment; emotional cruelty; regular violent acts toward people and property causing damage or injury requiring hospitalization or resulting in serious harm
5	5	

H10. Practical Judgement/Problem-Solving and Coping Skills

Refers to ability to develop options and make appropriate decisions/choices in areas such as child care, discipline, money management, personal relationships; ability to cope with daily stress. Also assesses awareness of own abilities and limitations.

STRENGTHS:

CONCERNS:

Caregiver Score A	B	Operational Definition
1	1	Uses excellent judgment; able to develop and build options; proactive approach to problem solving; has a variety of appropriate coping techniques; aware of and able to compensate for own limitations; excellent insight
1.5	1.5	
2	2	Generally good ability to problem solve and cope with stress; some ability to anticipate and develop options in advance; knows and works around own limitations; some insight into own problem-solving style
2.5	2.5	
3	3	Difficulty seeing options; makes good choices in some areas but not in others; some difficulty in acknowledging limitations; little insight into problem-solving style
3.5	3.5	
4	4	Poor judgement in many minor areas or one major area (e.g., leaves child with alcoholic friend); very limited ideas on problem solving and coping; difficulty seeing options even with help; no insight into own problem-solving style
4.5	4.5	
5	5	Grossly inappropriate judgment; unable to develop options to solve problems; unable to cope with daily stress; denial of own limitations

H11. Meets Emotional Needs of Self/Child

Refers to healthy balance between meeting own needs and child(ren)'s needs.

STRENGTHS:

CONCERNS:

1	1	Maintains healthy balance between own and child(ren)'s needs
1.5	1.5	
2	2	Some imbalance at times; marital relationship sometimes gets lost in family and child(ren)'s needs; child(ren)'s needs occasionally secondary to parent's, but causes no harm
2.5	2.5	
3	3	Frequently meeting own needs first with some emotional consequence but no physical consequence to child(ren) (e.g., mother rushes child(ren) so she can see boyfriend), uses child(ren) to avoid being alone; uses child(ren) for emotional support
3.5	3.5	
4	4	Pattern of meeting own needs first with potential endangerment (e.g., leaves latency age child(ren) in charge of toddler); refuses to acknowledge special needs child to the child's detriment; overly self-sacrificing ("My whole life is these children", "I do everything for them", "I am nothing without them")
4.5	4.5	
5	5	Meets own needs at expense of child(ren)'s emotional, physical, or medical welfare and child(ren) is currently suffering due to this

H12. Self-Esteem

Refers to current feelings about self.

STRENGTHS:

CONCERNS:

1	1	Able to make positive self comments; likes self
1.5	1.5	
2	2	Tends to be self-critical but can take positive feedback
2.5	2.5	
3	3	Low self-esteem; difficulty taking positive feedback
3.5	3.5	
4	4	Consistently self-deprecating; cannot identify positive in self
4.5	4.5	
5	5	No self-esteem; self-hatred

Behavioral Concerns/Observation Checklist

I. ACTING OUT BEHAVIORS:

BEHAVIORS EXPRESSED TOWARD SOMEONE OR SOMETHING OUTSIDE OF THE CHILD

Reported By:

Staff *Caregiver*

		Behavior	*Behavior Description*
		Poor Sibling and Peer Relationship(s) CHILD(REN): _____ NOTES:	Fighting, arguing, ignoring each other, being excessively competitive, destroying each other's things, belittling, dominating, and submitting. Ask which child(ren) has the problem, how it is manifested, how long it has occurred, what makes it better or worse, who may be the instigator, is problem with the same age peers, or older or younger playmates, or at school or in the neighborhood.
		Aggressive/Assaultive/Destructive CHILD(REN): _____ NOTES:	Physical expressions of feelings in the form of hitting with hands or objects, poking, pinching, biting, kicking, and breaking or destroying things. Ask who is the object of the assault, physical harm caused, objects used, what is destroyed, and how badly.
		Tantrums CHILD(REN): _____ NOTES:	Child(ren) yelling, screaming, kicking, banging their heads, biting, laying on the floor kicking, or any combination of these after a caregiver has asked for a behavior or refused something. Ask what sets the tantrum off and what the caregiver is currently doing when the child(ren) tantrums.
		Sexual Acting Out CHILD(REN): _____ NOTES:	Any inappropriate sexual behavior shown or done to another person, animal, or thing, including inappropriate exposing of private parts, inappropriate touching or fondling of another child's or adult's private parts, any actual or attempted penetration or oral contact with another person's private parts, or actual or attempted directing of another child to do any of these things to the child in question. Ask when this was first noticed, who is included with the child in the activity, and type of behavior shown.
		Run Away CHILD(REN): _____ NOTES:	Child(ren) actually leaving the home with the expressed wish to live elsewhere. Ask what prompted the running away and how the caregiver(s) has reacted.

Reported By:

Staff   *Caregiver*

		Behavior	*Behavior Description*
		Lying/Stealing CHILD(REN): _____ NOTES:	Not telling the truth and/or taking things of others. Ask what the child(ren) lies about and to whom, and what the child(ren) takes and from whom.
		Stubborn/Oppositional/Disobedient CHILD(REN): _____ NOTES:	Child(ren)'s resistance to control, needing a number of requests and maybe severe consequences to comply, resisting day-to-day activities like dressing or eating, and refusing to comply with requests. Ask when it occurs, over which issues, with whom, etc.

J. INNER-DIRECTED BEHAVIORS:

THOSE BEHAVIORS, SOMETIMES HARDER TO DETECT, IN WHICH THE CHILD'S SYMPTOMS ARE DIRECTED INWARD

Reported By:

Staff *Caregiver*

		Behavior	Behavior Description
		Sleep Disturbance CHILD(REN): _____ NOTES:	Any problem in falling asleep, staying asleep, waking early, sleepwalking, night terrors or nightmares. Ask when it began, which problem the child(ren) has, how often it occurs, etc.
		Somatic-Eating Problems CHILD(REN): _____ NOTES:	Any problem concerning digestion and eating, including eating too much, too little, apathy regarding meals, and eating too fast or too slow. Ask which foods or occasions are a problem and any medical consultation sought, etc.
		Self-Destructive/Accident Prone CHILD(REN): _____ NOTES:	A recklessness on the part of the child(ren) to normal concerns about safety, depending on the age and understanding of child(ren), and actual accidents the child(ren) has had. Examples of self-destruction include self-mutilation in the form of biting or scratching; banging body parts, e.g., head on a hard surface; trying to run across the street to beat cars; climbing too high or too precariously; playing with matches or other dangerous things, etc.
		Depressed/Withdrawn/Suicidal CHILD(REN): _____ NOTES:	Depression is difficult to diagnose in children because they may not show the same symptoms as adults. Do note any obvious lethargy, disinterest, withdrawal from human contact, sadness, tearfulness, preoccupation with morbid thoughts, changes in eating or sleeping habits, any behaviors that are obviously life threatening, threats of killing self, extreme depressions, despondency, preoccupation with death, etc. Ask what the family has done and to what extent the child(ren) has carried out any life-threatening acts.
		Anxious/Fearful CHILD(REN): _____ NOTES:	Child(ren)'s verbal and nonverbal cues of fear or anxiety including nail biting, retreating, repetitive gestures, twisting hair, or clothing, etc.

Reported By:

Staff *Caregiver*

		Behavior	*Behavior Description*
		Excessive Masturbation or Preoccupation with Sexual Parts CHILD(REN): _____ NOTES:	Whether this is a real problem or a caregiver's overreaction to it, see if the caregiver reports a concern; ask when, where, and how often the child(ren) masturbates or if the child(ren) inserts objects into vagina or rectum.
		Indiscriminate Attaching/Overly Friendly CHILD(REN): _____ NOTES:	Inappropriate (for age or developmental status) approaching, talking to, touching, or going with strangers or the worker.
		Encorpesis/Enuresis CHILD(REN): _____ NOTES:	Lack of bowel or bladder control unexpected for age, or deliberate release of bowels or bladder inappropriately. If enuresis, ask if child(ren) was ever dry, if wets day or night, when in day or night, if it has been reported to a doctor, and if any physical causes have been ruled out. If encopresis, ask if child(ren) was ever bowel trained; for how long; when soiling occurs, does child(ren) ever defecate in potty; diet; medical attention; home cures, etc.
		Lacks Spontaneity CHILD(REN): _____ NOTES:	An inhibited, rigid child(ren) who does not engage in fantasy play or fantasy talk, or who seems afraid of making a mistake.

K. SCHOOL BEHAVIOR PROBLEMS

Reported By:

Staff *Caregiver*

		Behavior	Behavior Description
		Learning Delays CHILD(REN): _____ NOTES:	If child(ren) has repeated a grade (including kindergarten), is struggling with grade work, gets poor grades, has had an evaluation at school or I.E.P., or is in a special class for delay. See if you can get specific information from the school, including a copy of the I.E.P. (the caregiver should have a copy).
		Disruptive in Class CHILD(REN): _____ NOTES:	Child(ren) takes the teacher's attention from other children, has been referred for testing, or is in a special class because of behavior. Ask what the child(ren) does to disrupt.
		Attended Many Schools CHILD(REN): _____ NOTES:	Depends on age and grade of child(ren); any midyear changes are significant, and 2 or 3 changes by 6th grade can add to already-existing school problems.
		Poor School Attendance/Phobia CHILD(REN): _____ NOTES:	Ask if you can see child(ren)'s report cards; note number of absences per days in semester. Ask about reasons for absences. If illness is reported, investigate validity. Look for overly close dependence of caregiver and child(ren).

L. HEALTH AND DEVELOPMENT PROBLEMS:

THE INTERVIEWER MAY WANT TO START OUT BY ASKING QUESTIONS REGARDING OVERALL HEALTH AND DEVELOPMENTAL STATUS, AND THEN PROCEED TO SPECIFIC QUESTIONS.

Reported By:

Staff	Caregiver	*Behavior*	*Behavior Description*
		Health Problem(s)—Chronic CHILD(REN): _____ NOTES:	Ask about long-standing conditions like asthma, allergies, skin rashes, digestive ills, and heart defects. Ask about onset, current medications, medical procedures, ongoing medical care. Attend to anything that does not seem normal (e.g., wheezing, odd posturing or way of walking, skin color, weight, height, crossed or wandering eyes, oddly shaped ears, etc.).
		Health Problem(s)—Current CHILD(REN): _____ NOTES:	Ask about recent illnesses, flu, fevers, colds, childhood diseases. Ask how these were treated by the family and if medical attention was sought. Look for lethargy, color, temperature of skin, weight, and height.
		Dental Problems CHILD(REN): _____ NOTES:	Observe the child(ren)'s teeth, look for missing teeth, badly decayed front teeth (baby bottle syndrome), tongue thrust (tongue protrudes forward during speech), misalignment. Ask if child(ren) has seen the dentist. Ask also about teeth brushing and frequency of sweets.
		Developmentally Delayed/Mentally Retarded CHILD(REN): _____ NOTES:	Ask the caregiver(s) if they have any concerns, at which level they think the child(ren) is functioning, major milestones (i.e., walking, speech), comparisons with siblings. Ask about school performance and reports. Observe the child(ren) closely, especially infants, toddlers, or preschoolers.
		Adopted CHILD(REN): _____ NOTES:	There is a higher incidence of maladjustment among adopted children. Ask when the child(ren) was adopted, why the family chose adoption, and what they know of the child(ren)'s history.

Reported By:

Staff *Caregiver*

		Behavior	**Behavior Description**
		Premature Labor/Difficult Pregnancy or Delivery CHILD(REN): _____ NOTES:	Ask how premature the child(ren) was (term +40 weeks), birth weight, Apgar scores, condition at birth, hospital treatment (e.g., respirator, jaundice), age at discharge. Ask about prenatal care, medications or drugs during pregnancy, bleeding, premature rupture of the membranes, type of presentation (head v. feet first), type of delivery (vaginal v. C-section), fetal distress.
		Asthma CHILD(REN): _____ NOTES:	Ask about age of onset, medications, emergency procedures, current physician care, type and severity of symptoms, frequency, duration, and how the caregiver handles this stress.

M. TEMPERAMENT:

A STYLE OF THINKING, BEHAVING, AND REACTING THAT CHARACTERIZES AN INDIVIDUAL. UNDERSTANDING A CHILD'S TEMPERAMENT HELPS A CAREGIVER KNOW HOW TO RESPOND TO THE CHILD EFFECTIVELY AND HOW TO HELP OTHERS, SUCH AS TEACHERS, UNDERSTAND THE CHILD. *The following are four temperament characteristics to discuss with caregivers.*

Reported By:

Staff	Caregiver	*Behavior*	*Behavior Description*
		Shy (*Introverted*) v. Outgoing (*Extroverted*) CHILD(REN): _____ NOTES:	A shy child has a more difficult time meeting new people or entering new situations, like child care or school. A shy child may hide from new people, fuss a lot in new situations, or be afraid to try to new things. An outgoing child smiles and laughs around new people, explores new places, enters new situations easily, joins other children in play, i.e., at a park. Look for child's ability to separate from caregiver, dress, care for self or complete tasks that other children of the same age do. Look to see if caregiver rewards dependent behavior or encourages independence. (Note: children age 6–30 months often fuss if separated from caregiver; 3–6 year olds are often shy with strangers).
		Activity Level CHILD(REN): _____ NOTES:	Many caregivers think their toddlers and young children are hyperactive. Observe for yourself. Ask if activity level varies with what child is doing. Can child sit through a meal? Sit still for a story or song or movie? Does child fidget, swing, legs, gesture with hands, always seem in motion? Does school report the same problem? Has a doctor been consulted and/or medication prescribed (which medicine and dose)? Some children tend to run v. walk, prefer running and jumping games v. sitting games, prefer quiet activities like crafts, reading, or looking at pictures. What are the child's preferences? Is the child impulsive, acts without thinking, i.e., run into the street without looking, take risks, accident prone?
		Attention Span/Persistence CHILD(REN): _____ NOTES:	How able is the child to stay on task or stick with something that is difficult? Can the child work on puzzle or drawing until done? When learning a new skill, does child practice it for a long time? When a toy or game is hard, does child switch to another activity? Does child seem to get bored sooner than other children of the same age? Can child remain at tasks like other children of same age? Does child's ability to stay on task vary with the activity, i.e., homework v. play?

Reported By:

Staff *Caregiver*

Behavior	*Behavior Description*
Demanding/Irritable/Difficult CHILD(REN): _____ NOTES:	How intense is the child's mood and how negative? Does child cry a lot? Is child hard to comfort or calm down when upset? Does child stay disappointed for a long time when taken away from an activity the child likes? Does child protest loudly and for an extended period? How easily is child distracted when doing something wrong? Will child accept something other than what child wants, i.e., candy v. a toy at the store? From verbal or nonverbal cues of caregiver and your own observations, note frequency of crying, frustration, tolerance of the child(ren), frustration of the caregiver, reactivity level of the child(ren) (e.g., overreacts to slight stimuli), fussing in infants, colic.

Service Plan and Closing Summary

Service Plan

CASE # _____   WORKER _____   PROGRAM/OFFICE _____

1. Problem: _____

      Rating

_____

      _____

     Goal: _____

      FAF Item #

_____

      _____

   Method: _____

_____

_____

2. Problem: _____

      Rating

_____

      _____

     Goal: _____

      FAF Item #

_____

      _____

   Method: _____

_____

_____

3. Problem: _____ Rating

_____ _____

     Goal: _____ FAF Item #

_____ _____

   Method: _____

_____

_____

4. Problem: _____ Rating

_____ _____

     Goal: _____ FAF Item #

_____ _____

   Method: _____

_____

_____

5. Problem: _____ Rating

_____ _____

     Goal: _____ FAF Item #

_____ _____

   Method: _____

_____

_____

Estimated Duration of Service: _____ Estimated Frequency of Contact: _____

Closing Summary

CASE # _____   WORKER _____   PROGRAM/OFFICE _____

Date Opened _____   Date Closed _____

REASON FOR CLOSING:

___ Family Completed Program Successfully
___ Family Moved From Area
___ Family Refused/Dropped
___ Worker Decided to Terminate Services
___ Other

OUTCOME ON GOALS:

Assessment Rating   *Termination Rating*

FAF Item #: _____   _____   _____

    Goal 1: _____

    _____

FAF Item #: _____   _____   _____

    Goal 2: _____

    _____

FAF Item #: _____   _____   _____

    Goal 3: _____

    _____

FAF Item #: _____ —

Goal 4: _____

_____

FAF Item #: _____ —

Goal 5: _____

_____

SUMMARY OF PROGRESS:

In your opinion, was progress made in this case? _____ Yes _____ No

Please specify: _____

_____

_____

_____

_____

_____

_____

In the family's opinion, was progress made in this case? _____ Yes _____ No

Please specify (Note: If not possible to ask family's opinion, leave blank): _____

_____

_____

_____

_____

_____

DISPOSITION/REFERRAL:

Did child(ren) leave home or go into any type of out-of-home placement? ___ Yes ___ No

If yes, please specify: _____

_____

_____

_____

_____

_____

During the course of service and/or at closing was the family referred for any of the following services? Check all services that apply. Indicate with a check if family received or is receiving the service.

SERVICE:	WORKER REFERRED	FAMILY RECEIVED SERVICE
Food	_____	_____
Shelter	_____	_____
Counseling	_____	_____
Day Care/Camp	_____	_____
Support Groups (e.g., AA, Parents United)	_____	_____
Job Training	_____	_____
Drug/Alcohol Treatment	_____	_____
Medical/Dental Services	_____	_____
Other—Specify: _____		

_____

_____

COMMENTS: _____

_____

_____

_____

_____

_____

_____

_____